D0942755

A Guide to
Peer Counseling

A Guide to Peer Counseling

Jewel Rumley Cox

JASON ARONSON INC.
Northvale, New Jersey
London

Production Editor: Elaine Lindenblatt

This book was set in 11 pt. New Baskerville by Alpha Graphics of Pittsfield, NH, and printed and bound by Book-mart Press, Inc. of North Bergen, NJ.

Copyright © 1999 by Jason Aronson Inc.

10 9 8 7 6 5 4 3 2 1

All rights reserved. No part of this book may be used or reproduced in any manner whatsoever without written permission from Jason Aronson Inc. except in the case of brief quotations in reviews for inclusion in a magazine, newspaper, or broadcast.

Library of Congress Cataloging-in-Publication Data

Cox, Jewel Rumley.
    A guide to peer counseling / Jewel Rumley Cox.
      p. cm.
    Includes bibliographical references and index.
    ISBN 0-7657-0153-7 (softcover : alk. paper)
    1. Peer counseling. I. Title.
BF637.C6C7   1998
361 .06—DC21   97-45908

Printed in the United States of America on acid-free paper. For information and catalog write to Jason Aronson Inc., 230 Livingston Street, Northvale, NJ 07647-1726. Or visit our website: http://www.aronson.com

To peer counselors everywhere
who so graciously give of themselves,
and to those who courageously accept
and use this gift
to foster their own healing and growth.

Contents

— *Introduction* —

Why This Book Was Written

For the past twenty years I have worked as a volunteer in various community agencies. These agencies include a drug abuse prevention center, women's center, crisis line, and churches. While my work focused on peer counseling, it also included referring clients to other community agencies and professionals, facilitating support groups, giving workshops, handling emergencies, serving on planning committees, and training other volunteers to do peer counseling and referring. During this time, working a few hours each week, I have peer-counseled thousands of troubled women and men. They brought to me every problem you can imagine and some you probably cannot imagine.

I have seen wonderful caring put into action directly by staff and volunteer peer counselors and indirectly by those who funded these nonprofit organizations. Although many of the volunteers with whom I worked were effective, some were not. Those who were ineffective seemed neither to enjoy their work nor to stay long with the agency. Most of the volunteer agencies where I worked had a high volunteer turnover. Some of the short-term volunteers were students serving internships during graduate work, the temporarily unemployed filling their time between jobs, and volunteers who, after working a short time, moved to another part of the country. However, I believe a significant proportion of the high turnover resulted from inadequate volunteer training. Poor training contributes not only to volunteer dissatisfaction but also to clients being inadequately served and resources being wasted in recruiting and training new volunteers.

One reason for inadequate volunteer training is that volunteer agency staff usually are overworked. Their multiple day-to-day operational tasks, including the colossal job of fund raising, leaves them little time to develop training plans. Most are forced to devise a training agenda quickly, using the only materials available to them: those written *by* professional therapists *for* professional therapists. However, because peer counseling, which is done by lay persons, differs from professional therapy in several significant ways, successful and appropriate peer counselor training must address a totally different set of goals and objectives. Thus these readily available professional materials are unsuitable for peer counselor training.

In most agencies that use peer counselors, training sessions are held about twice each year with additional emergency sessions held as needed to replace volunteers who leave. Professional therapists from the community often are drafted as training lecturers. There generally is little consistency from one series of training sessions to the next. Often the head trainer (the staff person or volunteer who plans and oversees the training) takes the prior training plan and revises it based on perceived but unverified needs, availability of training resources, and personal whims. The result of this process generally is that training plans simply evolve over the years with some of the needed basic skills being hurried over or left out altogether. Many of the training sessions I have attended (including some in which I served as one of the trainers) provided only a smattering of basic peer counseling skills and the philosophy supporting those skills. Instead the training program categorized clients as, for example, "the lonely and depressed," "drug abusers," or "the bereaved," and described the classic symptoms of those in each category. In my encounters with troubled people, I have found that individuals rarely fit neatly into any of these specific categories and, even if they did, knowing something of the characteristics of those in a particular category did little to provide me with the skills needed to respond to the client appropriately and helpfully.

I believe I am in a position to know what peer counselor training content and format works—and what does not work. This expertise comes from my thousands of hours with clients and my attending numerous training sessions at each of the agencies with which I worked. These training sessions included an intensive two-week, sixty-hour training course conducted by Stephen Ministries (an international organization whose purpose is to train lay church members to counsel their peers) and a peer counseling community drug abuse training program administered by graduate students at Florida State University. My most valuable experience, however, comes from my developing and leading peer counselor training for two years at a women's center. I developed a basic training plan utilizing my experience in doing the job, my firsthand observation of how new volunteers were trained, my observation of how the volunteers performed following their training, and the results of later follow-up interviews with the volunteers regarding how they considered their training to have been appropriate and inappropriate. My basic training plan emphasized skills needed to do the job and the philosophy supporting these skills. Over the two-year period, I made minor revisions to the plan to improve communication of these skills and philosophy.

Peer counselor training rarely, if ever, is approached from a "job analysis" point of view. Emphasis generally is placed on what has been presumed to be the "nice to know" rather than on the actual on-the-job requirements of successful peer counseling. For this reason, I have attempted in this book to address what I believe to be a real and widespread need for peer counselor training to provide structure and form based on well-thought-out goals and objectives. The book is based first on my observations regarding what a peer counselor *does* when he or she successfully counsels a women's centers, men's centers, battered women's assistance centers, drug information and treatment centers, missing person centers, sexual assault/rape lines, churches that use lay ministries, crisis lines or "hot lines," family services, and any other agency providing face-to-face or telephone volunteer peer helping.

Although the information in this book is directed toward peer counseling activities in an agency setting, it also should be useful to professionals in various fields who wish to gain greater proficiency in communicating with their customers, clients, or patients. Examples of professionals who might find this information helpful are attorneys, physicians and other health-care professionals, retail salespersons, hairdressers, and bartenders—the list is endless.

Also, individuals who wish to help a troubled friend or relative should find the information in this book helpful in learning what to say and when to say it—and what to avoid saying.

Can Peer Counseling Be Taught?

While it is true that some individuals seem to have a natural inclination toward being good listeners and supportive counselors, many do not. However, there is strong evidence that the necessary counseling skills can be taught if the basic attitudes and value system are present. Alan Keith-Lucas, distinguished Alumni Professor Emeritus at the School of Social Work, University of North Carolina at Chapel Hill, in speaking of volunteers, private citizens, and those in professions such as vocational guidance, probation counseling, and welfare work, addressed the question of whether or not the helping process can be taught.

> How much this process can be taught is a question to which we have no definite answer. Certainly its major principles can be set forth in logical form and to this extent it can be thought of as a communicable science, although obviously one in its infancy. At the

same time it must be recognized that its practice requires both experience and the acquisition of a considerable self-discipline. In this respect, it is perhaps an art but not an art that operates without structure and form and that cannot be analyzed. [1986, p. 19]

While there is considerable doubt that the basic value system underlying nondirective peer counseling can be taught in the short time span of a typical peer counseling training course, I certainly agree with Keith-Lucas that the basic principles of peer counseling can be set forth in logical form. Successful peer counselor training addresses specific nondirective skills: *what* to say when responding to a client who has poured out his or her troubles.

Is Peer Counseling for You?

Peer counseling is not for everyone. Because of the required commitment of time and energy, learning the necessary skills is not a priority for many. Also, nondirective helping requires patience and insight. Some people seem to have a natural abundance of these traits; others do not. Furthermore, in order to give nondirective support, a particular set of attitudes is essential. Not everyone has these attitudes. While new information received in peer counselor training may effect some change in a trainee's attitude, a major change is unlikely. Nondirective helping requires a nonjudgmental attitude toward others and a general optimism toward life. It requires a belief that problems are challenges that present growth opportunities and that each person has the basic potential to find his or her own answers and handle his or her own problems. It requires a warm feeling toward others. It requires an *absence* of a driving, "fix-it," action-oriented attitude and the need to build one's own ego by fixing other people's problems. Examining yourself in the light of these requirements may be useful to you in deciding whether or not you wish to learn how to peer counsel.

Organization of This Book

Agencies that provide peer counseling often are a "first stop" or a "first phone call" for those in need who do not know where to turn. One of the things a peer counselor does is to assess a client's need. Often a client's major need is simply to be listened to and supported during a crisis—a life transition. Peer counseling, which is essentially nondirective, fills that need. A large portion of this book (Chapters 1 through 6) addresses basic peer counseling skills (what to say and when to say it). Chapter 7 is devoted to common roadblocks to effective counseling (what *not* to do or say).

Another related skill needed by the peer counselor is how to effectively refer the client to needed services of another agency or professional. Chapter 8, "Other Things You Need to Know," covers this and other topics that build on the basic skills covered in the earlier chapters. This chapter also covers how the peer counselor protects the clients, co-workers, and him- or herself by maintaining confidentiality.

Although telephone counseling is similar in many ways to face-to-face counseling, some needed skills are unique to telephone counseling. These are discussed in Chapter 9.

Sometimes the client's needs are such that nondirective support alone is not adequate. If the client suffers from impaired thinking, is in an emergency situation, or is facing a terminal illness, additional skills are needed. These related skills are covered in Chapter 10, "Special Cases."

Notice that in the context of peer counseling the term *crisis* differs from the term *emergency*. A "crisis" in this context is a situation in which the client finds his or her usual coping skills to be inadequate. In this sense, all clients who seek peer counseling are in a crisis. Such crises usually are triggered by external happenings—a life transition. Examples of such crises are problems with interpersonal relationships, including marriage, dating, live-in mates, parenting, adjusting to an "empty nest," and relating to grown children, grandchildren, aging parents, co-workers, or supervisors; alcohol or drug abuse; financial difficulties; loneliness; depression; aging; terminal illness; grief; sexual difficulties; physical ailments; homelessness; incarceration; mental impairment; career stress or change of job; adjusting to retirement; stress related to high school or college; and unwanted pregnancy.

An "emergency," in the context of peer counseling, is a situation in which the client, or someone associated with the client, is in imminent physical danger. Examples of such emergencies are when the client is suicidal, when rape or other physical abuse has occurred or there is child abuse, and when there is a life-threatening reaction to drugs.

While, for clarity, the three major topics mentioned above—peer counseling, referral to a community agency or professional, and handling of emergency situations—are presented separately, in an actual counseling situation there often is considerable overlap. Some clients simply need support and a listening ear. Some need firm direction in dealing with a present emergency situation. Some need only information. Clients sometimes ask for information when all they really need is support and a listening ear. Or the client may ask only for support when he or she is in an emergency situation. Some clients need both peer counseling *and* a referral that will provide them further help or information. (Assessing client needs, a crucial peer counseling skill, is addressed in Chapter 8.)

Throughout this book, the term *peer counselor* is used to designate the one doing the helping; the term *client* is used to designate the one being helped (a client being helped by telephone is sometimes referred to as the "caller").

To manage my way around the dilemma of how to refer to the gender of the client or caller, I simply alternate, referring to the client as "she" in one chapter, and "he" in the next. I hope this will give somewhat equal time to each, or at least convince you of my intended impartiality.

Although it is impossible in a book of this scope to address all situations peer counselors may encounter, I have attempted to cover as many as possible and to give you a feel for the attitudes required to access your natural helping abilities so that you will be at ease in handling a range of situations.

The examples I give throughout the book are drawn from my experience as a volunteer. The names and situations have been changed, of course, to protect the privacy of the individual involved.

1

Philosophical Fundamentals of Peer Counseling

What If You Don't Know the Answers?

I have heard many peer counselor trainees say, "I'm not sure I know enough to be a peer counselor," their assumption being that, to help a client, one must have answers to his questions and solutions to his concerns. Although this is not the case, the assumption is not surprising. This is the way we, members of a scientifically oriented society, have been taught to get from here to there: recognize the problem, find the answer, and fix the problem. For many, this is the only known method for dealing with perplexities.

While a position as a peer counselor does include some non-counseling duties (e.g., referring the client to other agencies and handling emergencies) that require direct, straight answers, peer counseling itself is nondirective and, as such, does not focus on *fixing* the problem. A major segment of a peer counselor's time is spent doing *nondirective* counseling. You really do *not* need to have the answers!

Carl Rogers, the noted therapist, believed that "the most they [directive, answer-giving methods] can accomplish is some temporary change, which soon disappears, leaving the individual more than ever convinced of his inadequacy" (1961, p. 33). He summed up his nondirective approach by stating, "If I can provide a certain type of relationship, the other person will discover within himself the capacity to use that relationship for growth, and change and personal development will occur" (p. 33).

The intent of this book is to offer you ways to use nondirective peer counseling to provide the type of relationship that Rogers indicates is most likely to help the client help himself. Learning these peer counseling skills and putting them into action requires some understanding of why and how these methods work to achieve the desired goal. Thus this chapter describes the underlying needs of the typical client, how the needs probably came about, and why a nondirective counseling approach is most appropriate for helping the client to grow toward meeting his own needs.

How the Typical Client Views Life

The peer counseling client almost invariably has very low self-esteem. While the concerns clients bring to peer counseling sessions are many and varied, a continuing thread of similarity runs through them. My experience has been that virtually every client views life as a rather negative experience, not just his own life but life in general. In more extreme cases, he repeatedly says things like, "Life is no good," "There is no way to win," "Nobody cares," "Everybody is just out for himself," "I am getting what I deserve," or "There is nothing in life worth living for."

I hear in these statements not only expressions of the client's belief that he is unworthy, unloved, and incapable of dealing successfully with life issues but also indications of his perception of the world as a place that often is dismal, evil, and unfair. Also, as one talks with the client, it usually becomes obvious that the concern first presented by the client is not the only major difficulty in his life. From the client's seemingly negative perspective of life and the multiplicity of the concerns he presents, one begins to suspect there is a direct relationship between the presented concerns and the negative life perspective. The negative life perspective is probably not a result of the adversities the client has encountered; many individuals have considerably more significant adversities but still maintain a positive view of life and manage to deal gracefully and constructively with their hardships. It appears, then, that the client's presented concerns are symptoms of a deeper issue. In fact, from my many years of peer counseling with thousands of clients, I have come to the conclusion that, underpinning the concerns with which he currently is attempting to deal, virtually every client has a vital lack of both self-esteem and faith in the basic goodness of life. I have observed that the barrier between the typical client and his successfully dealing with his present problematic situation is his lack of belief in his intrinsic worth and value and consequently of the authenticity of his own opinions. The client often feels powerless and helpless. He does not feel affirmed as a valuable, worthwhile person. He has had little genuine affirmation from others. His family and friends, because of their own low self-esteem, come from a defensive rather than an affirming stance.

Perhaps we peer counselors can gain a better understanding of the client's somewhat negative self-image by considering the mechanisms by which the self-image is formed. While the exploration below is perhaps a gross oversimplification, I think it serves its purpose of providing you with insight into how the client arrived at his present view of himself and his world and how this impacts upon his solving his "problems."

A Look at Life's Beginning and Development

In infancy, humans are totally dependent upon others for their needs. In fact, as I understand it, at birth and for a short time afterward, the infant cannot distinguish between himself and his mother. As he grows and perceives himself to be a separate entity from his mother or other caregiver, he begins to make judgments about his worth. If his caregiver provides unconditional but "tough" love, saying "yes" to the child as the situation warrants, and a firm but loving "no" as the situation requires and the child's frustration tolerance level affords, the child perceives life as a positive experience and himself as a valuable human being. This early conditioning dramatically increases his chances of moving into adulthood with a high regard for his own person, a regard that is not unduly dependent upon the opinions and whims of others. On the other hand, if his caregiver neglects or abuses him, he is more likely to perceive life as a negative experience and himself as of little value. As he grows older and his "world" becomes larger, his view of himself is more likely to depend largely on how he believes others view his worth. He thus lives in a threatening world in which his view of himself is often dependent upon forces over which he has only limited control. Peer counseling clients typically have this latter developmental background in common.

Intrinsic Worth versus Pseudo Self-Esteem

The typical peer counseling client usually receives at least a minimal amount of approval from others. Unfortunately, most of this approval is usually based on what the *giver* of the approval considers important. This approval often confers on the receiver what I call "pseudo self-esteem," a feeling of conditional worth. Pseudo self-esteem is esteem based on status that, unless continually earned, will be lost. Examples are status based on career success, social position, wealth, power, athletic ability, health, youth, or physical beauty. If status is lost, the feeling of self-worth is lost. A person with only pseudo self-esteem operates from a position of desperate and defensive determination.

The motivation that drives a person to achieve can be based on authentic self-esteem (a sense of unconditional worth) or on pseudo self-esteem (a sense of conditional worth). The source of motivation is revealed when, for any one of various reasons, the person fails. Failure does not lower the self-esteem of the person whose self-esteem is based on a feeling of intrinsic, inherent worth. He simply sees failure as a challenge. When failure is experienced by the person whose performance is to feed his pseudo self-esteem, he falls apart. For example, if a person runs for political office because he wishes to engage his skills to make the country a better place, losing the election would cause disappointment but not devastation. (If he is extremely intelligent and has his head on straight, he might even feel a sense of relief.) If a person runs for office solely because of a need for prestige and power and loses, he is devastated. Dr. Joan Borysenko of Harvard Medical School said, "Most of us eventually will feel that life is out of control in some way. Whether we see this as a temporary situation whose resolution will add to our store of knowledge and experience or as one more threat demonstrating life's dangers is the most crucial question for the quality of our life and our physical health" (1987, p. 21).

Other Factors that Contribute to Low Self-Esteem

A number of other factors in our society contribute to the prevalence of low self-esteem. Some religious doctrines tend to belittle man, presenting humans as creatures who are born "sinners" who must appease their God before they can be okay. Some moralists teach that one must deny desires and passions in order to be worthy of life. Some philosophical theories contend that man is insignificant and that the universe, including man, is the result of an accident, that life has no inherent meaning, and that humankind has no intrinsic value. In addition, our culture is a competitive one in which many individuals and groups, intentionally or otherwise, feed their own needs for status and power by demeaning those whom they consider to be their competitors. None of these theological, philosophical, and social factors are great morale boosters! All of them contribute to a general cultural influence on the way one views life. And one's belief about the meaning of life (or that there is no meaning) has a direct effect on how one views oneself. It is a wonder any of us manage to have high self-esteem!

tion to love himself (i.e., have self-esteem). In other words, while the peer counselor does not provide in-depth therapy, he or she does attempt to provide an atmosphere that responds to the source rather than the symptom of the client's problem, responds to the cause rather than the effect. In a nutshell, the goal of peer counseling is *to provide an environment that is conducive to the client's better knowing, accepting, and loving himself.*

Those who feel skeptical of this goal and this approach might do well to consider that, in peer counseling, the alternative to affirming the client's intrinsic worth is to attempt to make him over in the peer counselor's own image.

The theory sustaining the skills taught in this book is that a peer counselor can best give the client unconditional love by nondirective counseling, which requires that the peer counselor embrace the ideas that (1) each person is uniquely different and special and each has a different set of values and lifestyle, (2) a person has the potential strength to solve his own problems and to work out his own life plan, and (3) affirming the client's intrinsic worth is more helpful than giving advice. Nondirective peer counseling is based on the further beliefs that troubles are inherent in life; facing difficulties can promote a person's learning, changing, growing, and evolving; and learning, changing, growing, and evolving is what life is all about.

Are You Qualified to Be a Peer Counselor?

Giving a client nonjudgmental, unconditional love is a tall order. How can we who do not love ourselves perfectly do this? If you are feeling overwhelmed by the implications of the requirements of attitudes and values necessary to be an effective peer counselor, let me encourage you. Although the attitudes and techniques presented in this book certainly would be effective in helping a loved one, offering affirmation to a client is in many ways easier. When we attempt to be supportive of a troubled loved one, our own needs and wants are usually involved and get in our way. We tend to become defensive when our own needs and wants are threatened. We are emotionally involved. When we support a client, however, our needs and wants are not involved except, perhaps, our need to be a successful helper. And let us hope that our desire to peer-counsel comes from our desire to be a positive force in the world rather than from our need to feel important by being a successful helper—the latter is more easily threatened. If we *are* working from a need to build our own self-esteem, being aware of our motivation will help us make allowances for it.

At any rate, if your philosophy is "in the ballpark" of the one expounded above, you are well qualified as a peer counseling candidate.

What Results Can Be Expected?

In general, people tend to grow slowly, if at all. However, it is well known that an individual who reaches out for help when he is suffering—assuming he is flexible enough to bend rather than break—is more likely to make use of offered help than is an individual who is not experiencing a crisis. A crisis often reveals to the client that what he thought was true actually is not. This dilemma promotes the client's receptiveness to new insights and his openness to new truths. Almost everyone can tell of a time in their life when they suffered diversity. Although they would not choose to go through it again, they are grateful for what they learned from the experience. I believe truth (reality) always contributes positively to the goodness, meaningfulness, and joyfulness of life—if looked at through the wide-angle finder, objectively, long range, so as to see the big picture.

One of my favorite comic strips was "Calvin and Hobbes." In one edition Calvin, sitting at his school desk, raised his hand and

or
You have all the responsibility but none of the authority, and
you may lose your job because of the inadequacy of the workers under your supervision.

Any response that restates the crux of what the client said lets
her know we heard but does not distract her from her train of
thought. When the client hears us restating her message, she knows
we listened and heard her correctly. Also, because we refrain from
asking questions, adding our opinions, or giving advice, she knows
we are believing and accepting her statements and are not judging the accuracy, appropriateness, or morality of her opinions. Our
nonjudgmental listening and restating will let her know we accept
her words as important and her as a person of value and worth.
Our acceptance of her will give her freedom to continue thinking
and verbalizing her thoughts without reserve. Feeling affirmed, she
will be more able to examine what she is saying and, where she
finds her logic faulty, will change her message to herself. We may
hear her contradict what she said previously. Our mirroring her
thoughts back to her demonstrates that peer counselors do not
offer answers but, rather, provide an atmosphere in which the client is better able to know, accept, love, and help herself.
Some new volunteer peer counselors protest that restating
what the client said is awkward. They fear the client will confront
them and demand to know why they are repeating what she said.
I have never had this happen. On the contrary, the client is so
absorbed in her present dilemma that all she notices is that she is
being understood. If a client were to question the peer counselor's
restating what she has said, the peer counselor could simply say,
"This is my way of letting you know I hear."
When we restate the content of what the client says, our tone
of voice is of utmost importance. Depending on our tone of voice,
the same words can communicate understanding, praise, criticism, or, with an inflection at the end of a sentence, a question.

For a demonstration of the criticality of the tone of voice in conveying the desired meaning, try saying to yourself the peer counselor's responses listed below using the tone of voice indicated in parentheses.

CLIENT: I'm going to a party this weekend.

PEER C: (*Restating*) You are going to a party.
- (*With praise, as in "how great!"*) You are going to a party!
- (*With criticism, as in "so you should be working but instead"*) You are going to a party.
- (*With an inflection at end of sentence, turning it into a question*) You are going to a party?

Some experts say that our tone of voice communicates far more than our words.

When peer counseling trainees first attempt to restate what the client says, most end their statement with an inflection in their voice. They tell me that responding by simply restating is such a new concept to them that, when they try to do this, they automatically form a question instead of a statement. Asking questions comes naturally; restating does not. When responding to content, questions are to be avoided.

Some successful peer counselors find it easier to let the client know they heard by prefacing their restatement with one of the following phrases:

"I hear you saying . . ."
"You seem to be saying . . ."
"If I am following you, you are saying . . ."
"I'm picking up that . . ."
"It seems to you that . . ."
"In other words, you are . . ."
"Correct me if I'm wrong, but I hear you saying . . ."
"From where you stand . . ."

"I heard these key ideas . . ."
"Let me see if I understand: you said . . ."
"What is emerging from all you said is . . ."
"Let's see, you are thinking . . ."
"Sounds like . . ."
"As you see it . . ."
"What I hear you saying is . . ."
"Your viewpoint is . . ."
"Your perception is . . ."

Using the correct tone of voice is especially relevant when using such prefaces. Otherwise the response could sound like an accusation rather than a restatement.

Even when the peer counselor succeeds in using the appropriate tone of voice to restate the client's message, he or she will find that concentrated listening is required to be able to paraphrase or summarize the client's statement so as to convey the exact meaning of what the client says. For example, the peer counselor may paraphrase or summarize what seems to him or her to be the client's chief message when, in fact, another message is the significant one. Consider the following example of the beginning dialogue of a counseling session:

SUSAN: All my friends have steady boyfriends and go out all the time. It seems like they're only interested in me as a backup. Like, if their boyfriend goes home for the weekend, then they know they can count on good old Susan. She's always home.

PEER C: You're saying all your friends have steady boyfriends and go out all the time and you usually stay home.

In responding thus, the peer counselor picked up that Susan was concerned about not having a boyfriend and not going out when, in fact, that is not what she said. The central idea in Susan's message seems to be how she believes her friends treat her. Something else may have been Susan's concern, but it is not the job of the peer counselor to analyze her statements. We need only examine what she says for its basic meaning and, as we paraphrase, restate the key meaning as accurately as we can. If Susan's concern is different from the one she stated, chances are excellent that she will get around to verbalizing her true concerns if we are patient and follow slightly behind her. An appropriate response to Susan would have been:

PEER C: You're saying your friends seem interested in you only when they cannot be with their boyfriends. It seems to you they take you for granted.

Here is another example of the fragility of the stratagem of simply letting the client know we heard without involving our interpretation.

JUDY: I'm so frustrated. My parents have been pushing for a nursing career for me for a long time, and that's what I thought I wanted, too. But this term I've really gotten into a math course and I've been thinking about trying engineering. It's really confusing, and nobody seems to be able to help me.

PEER C: It seems that nobody is able to help you decide whether or not to change your major. You are thinking of engineering but your parents are pushing you to pursue a nursing career.

JUDY: That's right. They've always wished I'd become a nurse, and there's nobody else to help me, and I need help.

Notice how, in her second statement, Judy picked up on the focus of the peer counselor's response (Judy's not receiving any help in her decision making) and put aside what originally seemed to be her (Judy's) main message (indecision about which field of study to pursue). The conversation now is directed toward Judy's need for help in making a choice. Her needing help *might* have been her major concern, but this is not the gist of what she said. By mentioning that she had nobody to help her, she might simply have been stating her reason for coming to the peer counselor for assistance. Look at the dialogue again and consider how the peer counseling session might have gone differently if the peer counselor had responded as follows:

JUDY: I am so frustrated. My parents have been pushing for a nursing career for me for a long time and that's what I thought I wanted, too. But this term I have really gotten into a math course and I have been thinking about trying engineering. It's really confusing, and nobody seems to be able to help me.

PEER C: You are having difficulty in deciding between nursing and engineering. Your parents have pushed nursing, and you thought that was what you wanted too until this term when you have really gotten into a math course. You are confused and have no one to help you decide.

In this response, the peer counselor, by reflecting the essence of *all* Judy said, sets the stage for her to work through whatever is on her mind.

In the latter response, notice also that the peer counselor adhered to Judy's terminology. Judy said she has "really gotten into" (a math course), and her parents have been "pushing" (a nursing career). "Really gotten into" and "pushing" could have a variety of meanings. Rather than asking Judy exactly what she meant, the peer counselor wisely incorporated these terms into her response. By doing so, the response accurately reflected what Judy's message meant to Judy and allowed her train of thought to continue uninterrupted. The real meaning of the terms probably will be revealed as Judy continues talking. If not, the peer counselor can learn later on what these terms mean to Judy, if necessary.

The ability to paraphrase the client's statement from the client's frame of reference requires intense, concentrated listening. The peer counselor's own frame of reference might result in an altogether different response. Consider this example of a conversation in the beginning of a counseling session.

SARAH: My son wants me to go to his school play. I know how important this is, but I just don't have time. I have so much I need to do. I lost my job yesterday. I need to write résumés and make some contacts.

PEER C: Your major concern right now is finding another job.

Sarah's major concern *might* be that she lost her job and needs to find another, but she didn't say that. Her main concern may have been dealing with the issue of parenting or, possibly, her inability to use her time wisely. Sarah may have wanted to talk about how to prioritize her time. Or Sarah's husband may have just left her, or she may have just learned she has cancer. The above statement may have seemed to Sarah a safer way to begin. At any rate, unless Sarah were unusually assertive (and most clients are not), her next statement, and possibly the entire counseling session, would have been about losing her job. And Sarah would have gone away feeling frustrated that she did not get to talk about her real issues. If Sarah were the exception and were unusually assertive, she might accuse us of jumping to conclusions, and she would be correct.

Sometimes, as was the case in Sarah's statement above, it is difficult to identify the client's chief concern. Until the client has talked for a while and the peer counselor has had a chance to get an overall view of her situation, the safest reply is to try to repeat the gist of everything the client said, or at least to focus on what appears to be the client's main concern. This takes our putting aside what would be *our* concern were we in that situation. Let us consider a response to Sarah that would have incorporated most of what she said:

SARAH: My son wants me to go to his school play. I know how important this is, but I just don't have time. I have so much I need to do. I lost my job yesterday. I need to write résumés and make some contacts.

PEER C: You consider going to your son's play very important, but you don't have time to go. You lost your job yesterday and you need to write résumés and make contacts.

A response such as this, with minimum deviation from Sarah's statement, would have left her free to continue with her own line of thinking. Further into the session, the client's concern will have been identified and the peer counselor's responses will not need to be so comprehensive.

Avoiding Reflecting Feelings

Responding to content does not include the peer counselor's reflecting what the client seems to be *feeling*. While reflecting feelings is an important skill (and is addressed in Chapter 3), in the beginning of the counseling session the peer counselor should respond exclusively to the *content* of what the client says. Let's look at another way we might have responded to Sarah.

SARAH: My son wants me to go to his school play. I know how important this is, but I just don't have time. I have so much I need to do. I lost my job yesterday. I need to write résumés and make some contacts.

PEER C: You are devastated about losing your job and you need to get busy finding another one.

SARAH: Well, no, what makes you think I'm devastated?

Perhaps the peer counselor would be devastated if she lost *her* job, but the client may not be devastated at all. She may be part of a big layoff in her company, may have expected it, and may even have welcomed it. Even if she were worried or devastated, she might not be ready to deal with those emotions. Certainly the beginning of the counseling session is not the appropriate time to reflect what emotions the peer counselor perceives the client to be feeling. Telling the peer counselor her story is much easier and less threatening to the client than getting in touch with her feelings. Before she can safely do the latter, she must have time to feel safe with the peer counselor; she must be convinced that the peer counselor is neither judging her nor planning to lecture her. However, if the client uses a "feeling" word, it is appropriate for the peer counselor to use that same word in her response—this is simply responding to content. In the conversation between the peer counselor and Sarah, if Sarah had said:

SARAH: My son wants me to go to his school play. I am so frustrated. I know how important this is, but I just don't have time. I feel so pressured. I have so much to do. I lost my job yesterday and I need to write résumés and make some contacts.

The peer counselor appropriately could have said:

PEER C: You consider going to your son's play very important, but you don't have time to go. You lost your job yesterday and you need to write résumés and make contacts. You're feeling frustrated and pressured.

Though the peer counselor uses the feeling words *frustrated* and *pressured*, he or she is simply restating the client's own words. Thus this response adheres to the guidelines for responding to content. Here is another example of the appropriate use of feeling words when responding to content.

JUDY: But what if I take a new direction and fail? It's so scary!

PEER C: Changing directions is scary for you.

JUDY: Yes! I feel panicky just thinking about it.

PEER C: You feel panicky when you think about taking a new direction.

Other Restating Responses

Summarizing the content of the client's comments each time she makes a statement would be awkward and unnatural. Another type of response that lets the client know we heard is simply to say "mm-hm." This response and others (e.g., "I see," "yes") that encourage the client to continue are generally referred to as *continuers*. However, if our natural way of inviting the speaker to continue talking is to say "I see" or "yes," we should make sure our tone of voice does not come through to the client to mean "I agree." Responses such as "mm-hm" say, in effect, "I hear you, I understand, go on talking." This is such an easy and natural response that some new peer counselors find themselves using it to the exclusion of paraphrasing the client's words. But responding with "mm-hm" all the time does not let the client know we heard. A more natural and effective method of responding to content is to interchange the two responses, sometimes restating

by paraphrasing and at other times responding with "Mm-hm."
Here is an example:

JEAN: Ever since I broke up with my boyfriend last week, I've
wondered if I did the right thing. I mean, maybe I was
too quick to decide. Maybe we really could have made it
together.

PEER C: You are wondering if you made the right decision about
breaking up with your boyfriend.

JEAN: Yes, I am. I mean he is a great person. I don't know, I guess
I was just so tired of our fights.

PEER C: Mm-hm.

JEAN: I miss him so much. I don't know if I just haven't adjusted yet,
or if I should have stayed with him. Sometimes we had such
good times together. But then we had these awful fights.

PEER C: You are remembering the good times—and the fights. You
don't know if your indecision is because you haven't yet adjusted to the breakup, or if you really made the right decision
to break up.

JEAN: Exactly! We are alike in so many ways. Maybe that's part of
the trouble. I don't know. I know our fights caused us both
to lose self-esteem, and then we fought even more.

PEER C: Mm-hm.

JEAN: I don't know. I just don't know which way to go. I don't know
my own mind. What can I do?

PEER C: I hear you saying you are reconsidering the wisdom of your
decision to break up. You are wondering if your present confusion is because you made a bad decision or because you
haven't yet adjusted to it.

JEAN: Yeah. I'm not sure I can know until more time passes. I know one thing though. I can't stand those fights! That's no way to live. Life's too short for that kind of misery.

PEER C: Mm-hm.

Summing Up

Responding to the content of what the client says is the least threatening response we can make. If done well, this type of response assists the client in pursuing her main concern. Hearing her thoughts mirrored back to her may give the client perspective and result in her rethinking her thoughts in slightly different ways. This also assures that the peer counselor will not lead the client away from what she really wants to discuss. Also, although the client's words may cause her to experience emotions about what she is saying, she will not be put in a position of having to deal with her feelings before she is ready.

Do not be misled by the seeming simplicity of responding to content. New peer counselors tell me this is by far the most difficult of all peer counseling skills to learn. One reason this manner of responding is difficult is because it is foreign to most people's way of responding to others in daily life. Most people do not respond to friends or relatives by restating their messages. Another reason restating messages may be difficult is because it requires that the peer counselor have a firm belief in the ability of each client to find her own answers, or at least accept that no one else can know for sure what is right for the client. I have been told by peer counselors who have not mastered this skill that they know they are talking too much or asking the client too many questions but are at a loss to know how to respond otherwise. It seems that peer counselors become convinced of the successful outcome of restating the theme of what the client says only after they have made a leap of faith and tried it. If a client is repeating herself as if she were trying to convince us her story is true, it may be because we have not heard or have not let her know we heard.

While it is easy to underestimate the *difficulty* of learning the skill of responding to content, it is even easier to underestimate the *value* of this type of response. Clients have said to skilled peer counselors, "I don't understand how you know what I am thinking," or "This is the first time anyone really understood," or "I don't know why, but I'm feeling so much better about myself."

Listening and responding to the content of what the client says contributes toward the goal of peer counseling, which is *to provide an environment that is conducive to the client's better knowing, accepting, and loving herself.*

3

Observing and Reflecting Feelings

Another skill required to be a successful peer counselor is that of reflecting feelings: the peer counselor's reflecting back to the client what he or she perceives the client to be feeling. Before we examine the "how to" of reflecting feelings, it may be useful to consider a definition of "feelings" and to contemplate some of the attributes of feelings.

What Are Feelings?

Our feelings are our emotional thoughts; that is, they are the psychical and physical manifestations of our thoughts. They are our perception of how some occurrence (e.g., the loss of a job or another person's attitude toward us) affects our well-being. Our present feelings may result from recent happenings or they may originate in data received long ago.

Primary and Secondary Feelings

Sometimes our present feeling is a mask for another feeling. Anger, for example, sometimes is a secondary feeling, one that masks more primary feelings of sadness or fear (Richo 1991). One feeling often is replaced by another because the replacement feeling is considered more acceptable than the original feeling. For example, we may find anger a more acceptable feeling than fear or guilt because we can be angry at someone else. Our belief that the other person is the cause of our anger frees us from having to take responsibility for it. Feelings of fear and guilt on the other hand would point the finger directly at us, leaving us responsible for handling the feelings. A "replacement" feeling may be substituted for the original one because the original feeling would hurt so much. Hurt doesn't hurt quite so much if we turn it into anger or frustration. For example, when we are turned down for a job, rejected by a lover, or experience the death of a loved one, our initial reaction may be anger, neatly bypassing the more painful original feeling of hurt.

Ambivalent Feelings

Sometimes we experience ambivalent feelings (two distinctly different feelings about the same event). For example, we may feel both happy and sad when our child leaves for college. This can be confusing and seem to defy logic until we take a closer look and realize that the event does indeed affect our well-being in both positive and negative ways.

Feeling Cover-ups

Sometimes we try to cover up a legitimate feeling by attempting to adopt an opposite feeling, one we believe society finds more acceptable. For example, some people act tough to cover up tenderness, or act sweet to cover up hostility, or put on a happy face to hide their sadness. Choosing to act out a feeling that is opposite to the one we truly feel may be done with complete awareness and intention or it may be an automatic and unconscious response formed by habit.

Denied Feelings

Sometimes we deny our feelings. If we have not become aware of them—brought them to the surface of our thinking, examined them, and defined them—they may reside more as a vague overall impression than as a specific feeling. When we deny our feelings, they may arise subjectively rather than through conscious mental effort, and may seem mysterious to us. Even when we are not completely in touch with our feelings, we may sense that something is "right" (we feel happy) or "wrong" (we feel anxious, frustrated, or depressed).

We may deny our feelings by ignoring them. We may think we are too busy to pay attention to how we feel. We may know intuitively that experiencing our feelings will be painful and we don't want to hurt.

An environmental and educational background focused on logic and reason may encourage us to give our exclusive attention to what we recognize as logical or "sensible." Our culture often tends to diminish awareness of feelings. Often there is a tendency to believe feelings are unimportant or that experiencing and expressing feelings reveals weakness, is foolish, or is morally wrong. Children are sometimes told that "big boys and girls don't cry," are threatened with punishment if they cry, or are consoled and told not to feel bad about their broken toy because another will be forthcoming. As adults, we are often discouraged from experiencing, and certainly from expressing, our feelings by being told: "Keep a stiff upper lip," "Don't cry over spilt milk," "You'll get over it in a few days," "Things could be much worse," or, simply, "Straighten up and snap out of it." "Emotional" women are labeled as "weak and weepy" and, of course, "grown men don't cry." Attempting to use logic to deal with feelings not only does not work but also usually causes us to feel threatened, to feel that we should not feel the way we feel. This causes emotions to intensify and often results in our attempting to bury them even deeper.

So we often deny our feelings because we believe they are not acceptable, and that if we express them *we* are not acceptable. The better we deny our feelings, the harder it is to regain the skill of getting in touch with them.

When we do not recognize and accept our feelings, we are demeaning their importance. We are telling ourselves our feelings don't count or that we need to hide our true selves. If this true part of ourselves is hidden from us, we tend to come from a defensive position and to react rather than respond. We may not be able to understand our own reactions. We may try to respond differently but find that we are unable to do so. If we try to keep the lid on our feelings, they may blow up at the most inopportune time. Trying to put strong feelings out of our mind only increases our reactions to them. Denying our feelings has a negative affect on our self-esteem and also can contribute to such physical maladies as ulcers, colitis, and hypertension.

Getting in Touch with Our Feelings

Getting in touch with our feelings is critical to our understanding ourselves. Only when we understand and accept our feelings are we in a position to examine them for accuracy, put the realized information in perspective, and go on to choose how we will deal with this information. If, in light of our present data, we see that our old way of thinking was erroneous, we can, if the thoughts tell us something negative about our well-being, breathe a sigh of relief in the knowledge that it is untrue. If these old, inaccurate thoughts tell us something positive about our well-being that is not true, we can face the facts and process our sadness or disappointment, grieve our loss, and get on with our lives. If our exploration concludes that the data that triggered the emotions are indeed true, then we can deal with this information consciously and choose how we wish to handle it. Only when we are in touch with our feelings can we really know ourselves and be in charge of our destiny.

Owning Feelings

It is important that we "own" our feelings. Most of us have heard others say, or have said ourselves, "She makes me so angry," or "He hurt me deeply." But our feelings are something that is going on with *us*; they are owned by *us*. Another person can create a situation that might contribute to our feeling a certain way, but their attitude or actions do not *cause* our feelings. Our feelings are *our* thoughts about the situation the other person created. Harriet Lerner (1985) says we become angry because our needs or wants are not met. She emphasizes that this is not to say our needs or wants are not legitimate, but that our needs and wants—and the anger experienced when they are denied—are owned by *us*.

It is hoped that the foregoing exploration of the term *feeling* will contribute clarity as we look at how to assist a client in getting in touch with his feelings.

The Importance of Reflecting Feelings

Unresolved feelings may be at the heart of the difficulty the client is having in understanding and resolving his problem. Before the client can deal with his feelings, he must recognize their existence. It can be very scary to work alone when trying to get in touch with and deal with one's feelings. It is much easier done in the presence of caring, nonjudgmental support.

As noted in Chapter 2, responding to the content of what the client says is very important and should be used to the exclusion of all other skills in the beginning of the counseling session or any time the client appears to be feeling particularly vulnerable. However, in a fifty-minute counseling session (and certainly in ensu-ing sessions) a client typically will tell the gist of his story and go on to tell how the events in the story affect him. For him to get beyond the initial relating of the story, it is not only appropriate but crucial that we reflect back what we perceive the client to be feeling. Our ignoring his feelings might convey to him that it is not all right to feel what he is feeling or that we do not care about him or are unwilling to support him while he delves into a deeper part of himself.

Some maintain that assisting a client in getting in touch with his negative feelings will encourage negative thinking. While his ruminating on or wallowing in his feelings might be detrimental, his simply becoming aware of and labeling his feelings is construc-tive. Often rational thinking is hindered by the pressure of pent-up feelings. Unrecognized and/or unexpressed feelings can cause tension and hinder the client's ability to identify and "work" on his problem. One way for him to relieve the tension of pent-up feel-ings is to talk about them. Pressure is relieved as the emotions are released. Our reflecting the client's feelings gives him permission to express them, helps him feel more comfortable with us, and cre-ates a closeness between him and us that enables him to trust fur-ther self-disclosure.

How Can We Identify What a Client Is Feeling?

After hearing the main theme of the client's story, we should begin reflecting back to the client the feeling we believe him to be experiencing.

How can we know what the client is feeling? Although the client's body language—his posture, his facial expression, the look in his eyes—might provide clues, they can be misleading. While it might seem that we could learn something about his feelings by asking ourselves how we would feel under similar circumstances, this actually is not a reliable method. He might not feel the way we would feel in a similar situation. And our asking outright what the client is feeling may seem threatening to him. He may believe he should answer but not be enough in touch with his feelings to do so. His words can tell us a great deal, however, especially if we listen carefully for the theme of his story. Most feelings, I have heard, can be classified as either "mad," "glad," or "sad." While I believe this categorizing to be overly limiting, it may help to evaluate the client's feelings. An even better indication of his feelings is his tone of voice. Do we hear anger, hate, joy, fear, or hurt in his voice? Is he enthusiastic about life, or is he dejected? By listening with our "third ear" and trusting our intuition, we must make an educated guess and reflect what we believe the client, from his frame of reference, is feeling.

When attempting to do this, we should neither focus on nor attempt to analyze what we think might be primary or denied feelings. It is out of the peer counselor's domain to probe in an attempt to determine the source of the client's present feelings—to ask him, for example, about events that took place in his childhood. The peer counselor is neither expected to have this expertise nor to take this responsibility. The appropriate role, rather, is to be aware of the importance of feelings, to have some understanding of the complexity of feelings, and to provide a safe atmosphere of nonjudgmental support so that the client, if he so chooses, can get in touch and deal with his feelings. Even when the client reflects what may be a secondary feeling of, for example, anger, this well may be a step in the direction of his getting in touch with his deeper feelings. After all, he must become fully aware of his anger before he is in a position to look at his hurt. In fact, after he fully realizes that he is angry, he may, on his own, begin talking about deeper, underlying feelings of hurt. Then and only then are we, as peer counselors, in a position to reflect the feeling "hurt." Our role and responsibility is to follow behind the client, accepting and reflecting his present feelings.

Why, then, is it helpful for peer counselors to be aware that the feeling the client is currently experiencing may not be the primary one? Our listening to a client express strong feelings can be very frustrating, especially if we cannot understand why he is feeling the way he is. Knowing that some feelings may be repressed and that the primary feeling may not yet have appeared helps me, at least, have the patience to follow along behind the client and address only his uppermost feelings. Also, if he expresses a particular feeling about some event and later expresses a completely different feeling, my awareness of possible causes of his ambivalence helps me accept and be supportive of his struggle for self-understanding.

Reflecting Feelings

After the client has provided the basics of his story, and aided by the clues noted earlier, it is imperative that we risk making a guess about what he is feeling and reflect this guess back to him. Here is a dialogue between a peer counselor and a client that incorporates reflecting feelings.

JOHN: I've been very ill and I just want to talk to somebody about it. It started a few months ago. At first it was off and on and wasn't too bad and I didn't think much about it. I could still work okay. And I am still working. (*Pause. A short silence*)

PEER C: Your illness started a few months ago. When it was not constant, you didn't think much about it. You could work okay, and you are still working. (*Responding to content*)

JOHN: Yes. I go to work every day, but sometimes it's very difficult because I feel so bad. And I know it will get much worse, and I don't know how I'm going to be able to continue working—to make a living.

PEER C: As it gets worse you don't know how you are going to be able to make a living. (*Responding to content*)

JOHN: That's right. And I don't know how I am going to be able to deal with the illness. I dread the pain. And I'll be alone a lot, and I'm so accustomed to being with people all the time.

PEER C: You dread the pain and the isolation. (*Responding to content. John has said he is in pain and, in effect, that he will feel isolated.*)

JOHN: Exactly. It's already showing up in my work. Last week my employer gave me this job to do, and I really tried. But I just didn't feel like doing it and I didn't do it well.

(*John talked about work for the next few minutes, and went into some of his job duties. The peer counselor alternated between responding by summarizing what the client said and using "mm-hm's."*)

JOHN: And of course I can't tell my employer about my illness or I'd be fired. I know him, and he'd fire me immediately. And I do want to work as long as I can.

PEER C: Your employer would fire you if he knew. (*Responding to content*)

JOHN: I suspected I had AIDS but I put off testing. When I did have the test, it confirmed that it's AIDS.

PEER C: The test confirmed what you suspected, that you have AIDS. (*Responding to content*)

JOHN: Yes. There are so few people I can talk with about it. (*John begins to cry, tries to continue talking, but cannot.*)

PEER C: (*Tenderly*) It's all right to cry. Take your time. (*This response is addressed in Chapter 8.*)

JOHN: It's so good to have somebody I can say all this to. I didn't know how you would feel about it. I wish I could talk to my family. My mother and father love me so much, and I love them, but I can't tell them about my illness. And some of my friends seemed to lose interest in me after I told them. And many of my friends I haven't told, but I'll have to soon.

PEER C: You feel isolated, lonely, and without support. (*Responding to feelings*)

JOHN: And you know what is funny? Actually funny? Having AIDS isn't my biggest problem. (*Looks at peer counselor as if he thinks she will ask him what it is*)

PEER C: AIDS is not your greatest problem. (*Responding to content*)

JOHN: My parents don't know I'm homosexual. They'd die if they knew. They feel so strongly. I simply can't tell them. If I stay around here, they'll know. I'm thinking of moving out of town.

PEER C: You believe your parents could not accept that you are homosexual. (*Responding to content*)

JOHN: I know they couldn't. But I want to be with them as long as I can. And I'm going to need their help. Tell me what I should do. Should I tell them?

PEER C: You want to be able to love them and experience their love for as long as you can. (*Responding to content and feelings*) You are wishing I could tell you whether or not you should tell them. (*This response is addressed in Chapter 8.*)

JOHN: Yeah. And I know you have no way of knowing how they would react. There are so many things I don't feel like I can handle. Work, my illness, whether to tell my parents. And I feel so bad much of the time.

PEER C: You feel pulled in many directions, and helpless, and ill. (*Responding to feelings*)

JOHN: You are the first one who has really understood how I feel.

Not all clients come to us with what may seem to us grave issues such as having a critical illness or becoming unemployed. But the accumulated stress of certain lifestyles can be just as much a threat to mental health. (Some sources that fund volunteer agencies who offer peer counseling justify this expenditure by considering peer counseling a preventative of mental illness.) Consider the following dialogue.

DEBRA: (*With anger*) I'm exhausted. I've had to do laundry every morning this week before I took my children to day care and went to work. And then after work, I have to pick them up, drag them around while I do errands, go home, cook dinner, supervise the children's baths and put them to bed, clean up the kitchen, and get my clothes ready for work the next day. It's that way every week, and do I get any help? Of course not! My husband just sits in front of the TV all the time. Says he's tired! He thinks *he's* tired!

PEER C: You're exhausted and your husband does not help you with the work. (*Responding to content*)

DEBRA: You got it! I don't know how much longer I can keep this up. I've only been working six months, but with the children now, we need the money.

PEER C: You don't know how much longer you can survive this pace, but you need the money. (*Responding to content*)

DEBRA: (*Calmer now*) The worst part is I'm afraid I'm not patient with the children. I mean I have so little time with them anyway. And we used to have a good marriage.

PEER C: You are concerned about your relationship with your children and with your husband. (*Responding to feeling*)

DEBRA: I just feel my whole life changing.

PEER C: Mm-hm. (*By compassionate tone of voice, responding to feeling*)

DEBRA: (*With anger*) After I work hard all day, he wants to have sex. Ha!

PEER C: You're too tired to have sex, and also you resent his not helping you. (*Responding to content and feelings*)

DEBRA: Yes, can't he see how unfair it is?

PEER C: You're feeling angry. (*Responding to feeling*)

DEBRA: Well, he did try to help when I first went to work. Said he would clean up the kitchen. Put the dishes in the dishwasher. Big deal! Didn't even wipe off the counter!

PEER C: You're saying when you first went to work, your husband tried to help with the housework, but that he did not do a good job. (*Responding to content*)

DEBRA: Yes. I came in to talk with you today because I see my marriage going down the drain and my children unhappy. Just now when you said my husband did not do a good job, I felt a little like defending him until I realized that was what I said. I know something has to give, and soon. And I know the way I have been criticizing my husband doesn't help anything. Can I come in again next week?

The peer counselor explained to Debra that she could come in for four more visits if she wished. Some clients have abundant resources within themselves to think through their dilemma and make changes, but are very limited without at least a minimum of support and a scheduled time and place to work.

    Notice, in the dialogue above, that the peer counselor said that Debra is *feeling* anger. Actually, Debra is temporarily experiencing feelings-thoughts of anger. Her whole being is not involved in her anger or any other feeling. There is a core part of her that is *observing* this impermanent feeling; this core will survive the feeling.

Dr. Jon Kabat-Zinn (1990), noted author, researcher, and associate professor of Medicine at the University of Massachusetts Medical Center, wrote:

> Rather than saying "I am afraid" or "I am anxious," both of which make "you" *into* the anxiety or fear, it would actually be more accurate to say, "I am having a lot of fear-filled (or fearful) thoughts." In this way you are emphasizing that you are not the content of your thoughts and you do not have to identify with that content. Instead you can just be aware of it, accept it, and listen to it caringly. Then your thoughts will not drive you toward even more fear, panic, and anxiety, but can be used instead to help you see more clearly what is actually on your mind.
>
> When you can successfully step back and see that you are not your thoughts and feelings and that you do not have to believe them and you certainly do not have to act on them, when you see, vividly, that many of them are inaccurate, judgmental, and fundamentally greedy, you will have found the key to understanding why you feel so much fear and anxiety. [pp. 344, 346]

The way the peer counselor reflects feelings to the client demonstrates the delicate but substantial distinction between the client's fleeting feelings and his core being. Rather than saying, "You *are* sad," a good response is, "You *feel* sad" or, even better, if the situation allows it without awkwardness, "You are experiencing feelings of sadness right now." This response sets up a framework from which the client can see his core self as separate from his feeling. While the knowledge of what he presently feels is extremely useful to him in getting in touch with what is going on with him at the moment, his feelings need not label who he is.

Here is a dialogue that further demonstrates reflecting feelings.

JIM: I'm having a very hard time these days. I just have to talk to somebody about it. I've done very well all my life. Just didn't know it could come to this. Still can't believe it.

PEER C: You have done well all your life and didn't know it could come to this. (*Responding to content*)

JIM: Yeah. It happened two months ago. Seems like a year. Things were going great at work, then bingo, just like that. Out of the blue. They laid me off. I didn't have time to think about it or anything. Once they let you go, you're out of there.

PEER C: Mm-hm. (*Responding to content*)

JIM: I knew it was happening in other companies, but I sure didn't think it would happen to me.

PEER C: It came unexpectedly. You sure didn't think it would happen to you. (*Responding to content*)

JIM: Yeah! A shock. I just can't handle it. I've asked around some about a job, but no luck. And I look in the papers. But mostly I just watch TV and try not to think. I feel like nothing, and I don't think anybody would hire me.

PEER C: You are feeling little and inadequate. (*Responding to content and feeling*)

JIM: Yes, I guess I am. And I felt okay just a month ago. It doesn't seem like losing your job would do that to you. I mean, I felt okay about myself then.

PEER C: Sounds like you're feeling confused. (*Responding to feeling*)

JIM: Yeah! You must see other people in this situation. Do they go down like this?

PEER C: You're wondering if others who lose their job feel as you do. (*Responding to content*)

JIM: Well, I know another man. A friend of my brother's. Said he just didn't have enough confidence to go out and look for a job. I know I'd better get the confidence soon or there won't be any food in the house. We don't have any savings. My wife works but she doesn't make enough to even pay the rent. And the children all need new clothes before school starts. I don't know what I'm going to do.

PEER C: You feel frightened. (*Responding to feeling*)

JIM: Yes, I guess I am downright scared. I don't know how to get a job. I mean, things aren't like they used to be—where you did your best for the company and you could trust them to be loyal to you.

PEER C: You're feeling betrayed and out of touch with the system. (*Responding to feelings*)

Usually, the feeling we reflect hits the mark. But even if our guess is inaccurate, the client likely will appreciate our efforts and use them constructively. Consider the following.

FRED: My girlfriend told me she didn't want to see me anymore. She's found somebody else.

PEER C: You feel hurt and betrayed. (*Reflecting feelings*)

FRED: No, I'm not really hurt. I've felt we were not right for each other for quite a while but I just couldn't muster the courage to tell her.

Only occasionally will a client show absolutely no recognition of the peer counselor's reflection. He may fear he is exposing too much of himself and feel threatened. If he seems uncomfortable or unaccustomed to dealing with feelings, a good response might be:

PEER C: Earlier we were talking about some strong feelings, and it seems our conversation has drifted away from talking about those feelings. I'm wondering if you find it difficult to talk about them.

If the client admits to feeling uncomfortable facing his own feelings, it may be helpful for him to discuss his feelings about his feelings. It is important that the client know we consider feelings important and are willing to hear how he feels. We should invite the client to deal with his feelings, but certainly should not prod him into doing so. If the client seems defensive, an immediate return to responding to content is in order.

Usually, if we have listened well and have refrained from leading the client away from what he wanted to talk about, he will use our reflection of his feelings as a means of discovering what he *is* feeling and thus will communicate with us on a deeper, feeling level.

Feeling Word Vocabulary

Having a good "feeling word" vocabulary enables us to choose a word that describes not only the client's feelings, but the intensity of the feelings. If the feeling "annoyed" is reflected when the client obviously is "infuriated," or if "sad" is reflected when he is "deeply depressed," the reflection will diminish his actual feeling and he will not feel understood.

At the end of this chapter is a list of some of the emotions a client might be experiencing. It may be helpful to make your own list, probably a much shorter one, that includes words you ordinarily use and feel comfortable with. In telephone counseling some peer counselors find it helpful to refer to such a list. A list somewhat by subject is reported to be more helpful than an alphabetized list.

Feelings and Logic

One cannot rationalize away feelings. Any attempt on the part of the peer counselor to apply logic to the client's feelings will usually cause him to feel threatened, to feel like he should not feel the way he feels. This in turn causes his emotions to further intensify as he becomes defensive. When the client asks us to listen and understand what he is feeling and we tell him he should not feel the way he feels, we are showing disrespect. We are trampling on his feelings. Responses such as the following should be avoided.

JIM: My supervisor tells me to do one thing and then, after I do it, he tells me I did it all wrong. My co-workers don't have a problem with him. I think he's looking for an excuse to fire me, but I haven't the vaguest idea why. I feel like I'm going crazy.

PEER C: Maybe your supervisor acts that way because he is having a rough time. Perhaps you are too sensitive or are taking it too personally.

When and When Not to Reflect Feelings

Reflecting a client's feelings can be threatening; reflecting the content of what he says is not. When we reflect what the client seems to be feeling, we may be giving him new data; he may not have been aware that he felt that way. While reflecting his feelings is of utmost importance, it must be well timed to be effective. Reflecting feelings is appropriate at any time during the counseling session except in the following situations.

• *At the beginning of the counseling session.* We should not reflect the client's feelings at the beginning of the counseling session. The session should begin with nonthreatening responses. Also, we are not in a position to make a considered judgment about what the client is feeling until after we have heard the client's story.

This true story depicts what can happen when a peer counselor reflects feelings too quickly in a conversation. Long ago, in an agency where I worked as a volunteer, a new volunteer apparently missed the training session on "Responding to Content" but learned well the lesson on "Reflecting Feelings." One of her first clients, very early in the session, told the peer counselor that her husband had died recently. The new volunteer, with great empathy, tenderly reflected, "You are so very sad and are grieving your loss." The client quickly responded, "Hell, no! I couldn't be happier that the S.O.B. is gone!"

I never did learn why this client came for peer counseling but, obviously, it was not to receive support in her grief. Had the peer counselor listened and paraphrased for a while, no doubt she would have been spared putting her foot in her mouth.

- *When the client is highly emotional.* Another time to avoid reflecting feelings is when the client is overwrought or is experiencing intense emotions. Perhaps he has just heard some shocking news, or possibly what has happened so far in the counseling session has allowed him to see reality more clearly. He may not be aware that he is experiencing strong emotions, but to have this pointed out would likely be overwhelming to him. In these situations, the appropriate responses are those that are the least threatening, those that do not offer even an iota of new data but simply allow him to know we hear. As we respond to the content of what he says, we can acknowledge his intense feelings simply by responding in a gentle and caring tone of voice.

I remember a new volunteer peer counselor who was talking on the phone with a highly emotional client. The woman on the other end of the line was obviously agitated and spoke with such a loud voice that I, a few feet away, could hear every word she said. She was recounting what her boss had said and was ranting and raving about how she had been unfairly fired from her job. The new peer counselor reflected to the woman, "You are very angry." The woman replied, even louder than before, "You're damned right I'm angry! Wouldn't you be angry if this just happened to you?" upon which she slammed down the receiver. She did not feel understood; she felt accused. When a client displays intense emotions of any kind, we can show sensitive support by responding only to the content of what he says.

• *When hurried.* We should not encourage a client to explore his feelings when we know our contact with him will likely be brief—for example, when we are talking with him on the phone to make an appointment, when he has told us he cannot talk long, or any other time when his processing of his feelings might be abruptly discontinued. To encourage him to process feelings at such times might leave him feeling frustrated or deserted when the discussion ends. If he begins talking about feelings at such times, we can tell him that what he is saying is important and should be discussed later when we are unhurried.

• *When terminating a session.* Feelings should not be dealt with when the session is being terminated. Attention to feelings when attempting to wrap things up would serve only to prolong the termination and leave the client struggling with feelings he did not get a chance to process. (More about terminating a session is provided in Chapter 6.)

Summing Up

People do not feel understood on a deep level until their feelings are understood. A well-timed reflection of feelings lets the client know his emotional viewpoint is allowed, understood, and not judged. Only after he has received affirmation that it is okay to feel what he feels will he begin to own his feelings. Accepting ownership of his feelings allows him to look at them objectively and provides him more control over his decisions and actions. Understanding what the client is feeling, and communicating our understanding to him, is truly a gift of caring. Reflecting feelings helps *provide an environment that is conducive to the client's better knowing, accepting, and loving himself,* the goal of peer counseling.

FEELING WORD LIST

uneasy	disgusted	depressed
nervous	resentful	downcast
alarmed	frustrated	unworthy
startled	angry	vulnerable
afraid	mad	
fearful	enraged	tired
scared	furious	tense
panicky	bitter	exhausted
jealous	irate	weary
trapped		ill
threatened	guilty	
terrified	remorseful	refreshed
petrified		relaxed
	surprised	
anxious	astonished	hopeful
bothered	shocked	relieved
concerned	lonely	peaceful
confused	isolated	safe
disturbed		free
unsettled	abandoned	inspired
vexed	rejected	
perturbed	betrayed	happy
troubled	hurt	glad
worried		delighted
upset	disappointed	joyful
distressed	grieved	elated
distraught	sad	
tormented	dejected	confident
horrified		courageous
	intimidated	adequate
annoyed	helpless	capable
irritated	defeated	proud
exasperated	inferior	loving
agitated	worthless	
provoked	diminished	

—— *4* ——

Assisting a Client in Exploring Options and Making Decisions

At this point you may be thinking that listening to the client, responding to the content of what she says, and reflecting her feelings is just too easy and will be ineffective in helping her address her concerns. You may think she needs help in solving her problems, that she needs advice, that she needs to be told what to do. If so, join the club! Most volunteer peer counselor trainees feel that way. However, as previous chapters have emphasized, peer counselors do not give advice. This rule has not changed. Assisting a client in exploring options and making decisions does not require giving advice.

Many problems seem to have simple solutions, especially if they are someone else's problems. If one of our friends is being abused by her spouse, why does she not just leave him? If our brother gets laid off from his job, the solution seemingly is simple: he should look for another job. If they do not implement these simple solutions, we have trouble understanding just what is going on with them. This chapter addresses this issue. A large part of it addresses (1) why we may desperately wish to offer our clients what seems to us to be obvious solutions to their problems, (2) why clients often are prevented from seeing what, to others, are obvious solutions to their problems, and (3) why giving advice is not helpful. The steps in, and some examples of, assisting a client in exploring options and making decisions is covered in the latter part of the chapter.

Why the Urge to Give Advice?

It is not surprising that attempting to fix the client's problem is the first thing that occurs to many peer counselor trainees. Most of us at one time or another have given outright advice to our relatives or friends either by going in the front door ("I think you should try this") or by going in the back door ("I don't know if this would work for you, but it sure did for me"). No harm is done to our family or friends—if they are free to take our advice or leave it. And no harm is done to us—if our family and friends are able to overlook our need to dish out advice and still love us as they did before.

Most of us address our own concerns by looking for solutions. Finding immediate solutions is what we think we want for ourselves, and fixing the problem is what we think we want for our client. At first glance it seems honorable to give of ourselves and our time to try to find an answer to our client's problem. But is it? Here are some obviously well-intentioned, though not particularly honorable, reasons why we might be inclined to give the client advice:

- Our need to "fix" might be based on our ego need to be a successful helper rather than on our sincere desire that the client come to believe in herself. When we are tempted to give advice, it behooves us to ask ourself whose needs we are addressing.

- Many of us are task oriented. We do not like to waste time. Refraining from giving the client the solution, which to us seems obvious, is very frustrating for us.

- We may be inclined to give advice because we are uncertain of our own values. The more unsure we are of our values, the more we are tempted to defensively try to impose them on others. Influencing others to think and behave in line with our values seems to provide evidence that we are right. If we find ourselves trying to substantiate our values by imposing them on others, we may want to take a close look to determine whether we inherited (or adopted) our values or thought them through for ourselves. If our values are truly ours, we will have no need to defend them or push them off on others.

- We may hand a client a solution so we will not have to hurt with her. A good peer counselor knows that he or she is not responsible for the client's life. Yet, being sensitive and empathic, he or she does hurt with the client, or at least finds the experience intense and tiring. Sure, we chose to be peer counselors, but some days we are just not in the mood to be empathic.

- We may not have mastered the more difficult skills of listening, responding to content, and reflecting feelings. If we have not, we may offer our client simple answers to complex problems simply because we know of no other way to respond.

We have a right to help—our clients have asked for help—but we do not have a right to control. Even if we use the appropriate peer counseling skills, our client may not be able to take advantage of the support we give, but that is not our responsibility. The client has a right to self-determination; she even has a right to fail.

A Personal Story

As a volunteer on a crisis line, I once took a call from an elderly man who was distraught. His children were trying to persuade him to go to a nursing home. They were close to attempting to declare him legally incompetent and forcing him to go. He was clearly unable to do a very good job of taking care of his own needs. He had difficulty getting his own food, wore dirty clothes, and often would forget to take his medicine. He sometimes would fall and not be able to get up until a neighbor happened to come by to visit him. He told me, however, that being free from pain or even continuing to live was not the important thing to him. He said he had lived in his house for over forty years and had loved his wife and reared his children there. His possessions were familiar. His ambitions and dreams were formed in this very house. His memories of fulfilling many of those dreams and ambitions dwelt there. And his faithful old dog was there. Would you have advised this man? If so, how?

Obstacles to Wise Decision Making

All of us, including our clients, are often prevented from seeing what to others are obvious solutions to our problems. Following are factors that can contribute to this inability to make knowing decisions.

- *A rigid attitude.* A rigid mental attitude may keep us from being creative in looking for options. We may be so set in our thinking that we assume there is only one "right way." There rarely is only one solution to a problem.

- *Strong emotions.* Our decision-making capabilities may be blocked by our emotions. If our well-being or desires seem threatened, we may become overwhelmed with emotions. Emotions block attempts to be objective.

- *Denial of the problem.* We may deny that we have a problem, or choose to be unaware. We may vaguely sense a problem but fear that facing it will require changes we do not wish to make. The possibility of having to give up what we currently believe to be reality (truth) in exchange for the unknown may cause anxiety and hence denial. We cannot deal with a problem if we deny its existence.

- *Faulty assumptions.* Faulty assumptions may contribute to unfortunate decisions. A client once told me, "I am too old for anyone to hire me." This may have been true, but I suspect it was not. Faulty assumptions may prevent our seeing good possibilities.

- *Inability to recognize limitations.* Then again, we may be unable to recognize genuine limitations of possibilities. Maybe our goals are too high, as I judge was the goal of the 94-year-old man who did not finish high school but planned to become a brain surgeon.

- *Intense desires.* Our desires may be so intense that we focus on what we wish would happen (which well may be a fantasy) and thus are prevented from considering legitimate possibilities.

- *Oversimplification.* We may oversimplify. I remember a client who insisted that because she liked to help people she should become a social worker.

- *Fear of failure.* We may be so afraid of failure that we hesitate to take the risk necessary to gain what we desire. This may cause us to disregard our true objectives and focus instead on some unrelated action in which we think we are likely to succeed. Or we may put off attempting to solve our problem until we have assurance that our attempted solution will work. Sometimes the data concerning the appropriate direction to take are 49 percent one way and 51 percent the other—and that is all the data we are likely to get until after the fact. Life holds no guarantees.

- *Refusal to "own" the problem.* We may refuse to "own" our problem: to exercise the freedom, power, and control that carries with it implied responsibility for the outcome of the decision. We may blame others or look to others to make the decision for us. We may choose to be unaware that not making a decision is making one by default.

- *Unrealistic value system.* Our value system may not be aligned with reality, and our misguided values may lead us away from constructive change. We may choose short-term happiness over long-term gain. We may not realize that life is more about growth than about happiness.

- *Rushing.* We may insist on immediate results. For example, we may try to control our weight by going on a starvation diet but be unwilling to adopt the lifestyle changes necessary to maintain the weight loss.

- *Unclear goals.* Our goals may be so numerous that we get confused and do not know where to start. We would do better to attempt only one major change at a time.

- *Pride or arrogance.* It takes humility to change. We cannot change until we admit that change is needed. We may not be willing to admit that we judged a situation incorrectly, were negligent or careless, or tried something we did not know how to do. The ease or difficulty of our changing may depend on the extent to which we place moral labels on our thinking or acting, or even on ourselves as persons. Recognizing our errors and using them as learning experiences is constructive; getting bogged down in guilt or depression is destructive.

- *Desire to avoid stress.* Even positive change can add to our responsibilities and be stressful. Consciously or unconsciously, we may wish to avoid this stress and thus make decisions that are sure to lead to failure.

- *Low self-esteem.* A low self-concept often is a stumbling block to change. Our low self-esteem may be the problem, in which case the stories we tell in describing our concerns may well be symptoms of the real concern. For example, we may define the concern as the inability to assert ourselves when the underlying problem is that we do not have confidence in ourselves. If we think well of ourselves, we are unlikely to have difficulty being appropriately assertive.

- *Failure to act.* Even if we have a self-concept of value and worth, however, these alone will not effect change. Achieving change requires not only a well-thought-out plan, but also self-discipline, willingness to act, volition, commitment, and tenacity; it requires spirit. There comes a time, a place, a particular moment, when, if we wish to change, we must gather our courage—courage we perhaps thought we did not have—and we must *act!* We must cease analyzing and planning and *move.* Spirit and tenacity may be what separates the women from the girls.

- *Assuming there is no solution.* We may believe we have no choices. Actually, we do have choices, although not necessarily ones that will completely satisfy us. There are two ways for us to effect change: change the situation, or change our attitude toward the situation. While the latter can be a pain-

ful and difficult process, our acceptance of the reality of
the situation can free us to explore ways to live constructively with it. Perhaps, though, with hard work, we can
change the situation. Acceptance may be chosen, not because there are no alternatives, but because acceptance is
the easy way out. As Reinhold Niebuhr's well-known prayer
says:

> Give us grace to accept with serenity the things that cannot be
> changed, the courage to change the things which should be
> changed, and the wisdom to distinguish the one from the other.

One or several of the above factors may be involved in pre-
venting the client from pursuing what seems to us to be an obvious and straightforward resolution to her difficulty. How are we
to make use of this knowledge in our peer counseling? Numerous
obstacles to good decision making are often ingrained in the client's
personality. A few hours of peer counseling are unlikely to bring
about major changes in these personality traits. Our being aware
of a little of the complexity of decision making, however, may help
us have patience with those clients who are not receptive to exploring options and making decisions.

A Firm Peer Counseling Rule

There are few firm rules in peer counseling. But in most agencies
that use such volunteers, there is one specific, strictly upheld, non-
negotiable rule. *Don't give advice!*

Whether or not to give advice is questionable in any situation.
In peer counseling it is not open to debate. The answer is an emphatic "no." Such an emphatic statement requires a rational justification, and I believe it has a solid one. There are many reasons a
client cannot use our answer to her problem. Following are the
major ones.

Why Giving Advice Is Not Helpful

- *The client is the expert regarding her situation,* and therefore is more capable than we are of handling it. She knows her resources and what she can put into action and what she cannot. She has more information than we do concerning her difficulty and its possible solutions. We simply cannot learn all there is to know about the client and her concern in the short time we are with her. A decision based on our values and lifestyle would be of little use to her because her values and lifestyle are different and she can work only within the framework of her own value system. Personalities are conglomerates of all past experiences and choices as well as genetic endowments. Humans are far too complex to ever fully understand one another, and their values are so different that what works for one would not necessarily work for another. If, by some fortunate coincidence, we managed to solve our client's immediate problem, we would not be with her to help her solve the next one.

- *The client has more at stake than we* do and therefore is more motivated than we are to think through and work on her difficulty.

- *We set ourselves up as an authority rather than a peer* when we offer advice. Presenting ourselves as authorities not only is inaccurate but also interferes with the helping process. When we offer advice, the entire relationship between us and our client changes; instead of its being a supportive relationship, it becomes a dependent one.

- *The client is vulnerable and may unwisely take our advice.* People who go to peer counselors for help are often easily influenced and may be accustomed to looking to others for direction. If we offer advice, our client just might take it without fully considering its impact. If she takes our advice and it does not solve her dilemma, she can blame us and not take responsibility herself. If by chance, our advice does solve her immediate problem, her dependency on others for answers will be reinforced. If *she* chooses which way she wants to go, she will be more likely to accept ownership of the problem and take responsibility for the outcome. In fact, she might get out of her rut and start a spiral of feeling more satisfaction, integrity, and self-esteem.

- *Permanent change usually involves an understanding of why we behave as we do.* Individuals rarely make permanent change through self-discipline. One good way for the client to learn why she behaves as she does is for her to get in touch with, explore, and become amicable with her feelings. Our attempt to force her to face reality when she is not in touch with the feelings that guide her is unwise and can also be dangerous, particularly since we cannot provide the skilled and ongoing support she needs to handle the reality. Our attempts to advise her bypass the process necessary for her to change her thinking pattern or ways of behaving. Advice, as with threats and persuasion, rarely changes attitudes and behaviors. If advice does effect change, the change usually is short-lived.

- *The present issue may be a symptom of the real problem.* For example, the client might believe her problem is that her boyfriend constantly belittles and verbally abuses her. You and I might believe her real problem is a lack of sufficient confidence in herself to prevent such happenings. The solution to the situation might seem simple enough to us: confront him and, if he is unable or unwilling to communicate and cannot or will not cease abusing her, dump him. However, our solution may not be her solution. She would have found her own solution had some barrier not prevented her from doing so. That barrier might be an unrealistic belief in her lack of value as a human being. She is probably not aware of what holds her back but may feel instinctively that she cannot afford the emotional or material price she would have to pay to follow through on what might seem to us to be a simple solution.

- *The client likely does not want advice.* Even if she asks for advice, she probably does not really welcome it. If she does welcome it, she may be open only to advice that does not require her to change in any way.

Another Personal Story

During my shift on a local crisis line, I once talked with a client we will call Lori who began by saying she called to get advice about a decision that must be made that day. She made it clear she phoned for one purpose only: to have me tell her what she should do—and quickly. Lori said her ex-husband was now living in another state. During the time they were married to each other, it seems, he had become interested in another woman, had divorced Lori, and married the other woman. Lori said she missed her man terribly and that the divorce was his idea. At that point she cried and, between sobs, said that she was falling apart and could not eat or sleep, that her emotions interfered with her work so much she feared losing her job. Lori phoned her ex-husband often and, in one of their conversations, he mentioned that his present wife would be away the following weekend. Lori asked if she could visit him for the weekend, and he said she could. Lori's explanation of her problem was that she had made train reservations to visit him the following weekend and today was the deadline for buying the ticket. If she bought the ticket, she would not have enough money to pay next month's bills. "Should I buy the ticket?" she demanded.

I responded to the content of what she had said. "Now, let me see if I am with you. You really want to visit your ex-husband who lives in another state, and you are trying to make an immediate decision as to whether or not to buy the train ticket because today is the last day you may do so."

She seemed to calm down a bit. Her voice was steadier. She talked some about their breakup. She restated how she missed him and could not make it without him. I reflected feelings: hurt, betrayal, loneliness, fear. Between crying spells she talked, this time about her feelings and how afraid she was of facing the future alone.

After she had told her story and gotten in touch with her feelings, I told her that talking it out really helps most people. I mentioned that most of us have times of transition in our lives when we need support, that we really do not have to carry the burden alone. I suggested the possibility of her going to a professional therapist for support during her time of crisis (in addition to using our crisis line). She said she would like to do so but had neither the money to pay a professional therapist nor insurance that would cover the visits. I told her about the affordable counseling available at the local county mental health department and at the women's center, explaining that there would be no conflict if she phoned us between visits to them. She indicated that she would like to do this and asked me for their phone number, which I supplied.

I told her we could talk a bit longer—that I had first wanted her to know continued support was available. She ended by saying a friend of hers told her she was crazy to think about visiting her ex-husband. She recounted that she must make the decision about buying the ticket that day and she did not know what she would do. Her words told me she was beginning to take responsibility for making the decision herself. Perhaps she realized I was not going to make it for her, or perhaps she knew she would not like, nor take, my suggestion even if I gave it.

I ended the call by telling her I knew it was a difficult decision for her. I wished her well and invited her to phone again. I don't know the outcome—peer counselors seldom do. I know only that she seemed stronger at the end of the conversation than she did at the beginning—somehow less desperate—and a lecture from me would not have helped.

Reflections

After I hung up the phone, I remembered a time in my own youth when I was in a crisis and my emotions had completely blocked my logic. I hoped the client perceived my empathy, respect, and optimism regarding her potential strength and ability to grow. Whether or not she visited her ex-husband or paid next month's bill on time probably was relatively unimportant in the overall scheme of things. I believed that her feeling my respect and good will and growing a bit stronger to be of more value than finding a solution to her immediate quandary.

When we do for a client what she can do for herself, we contribute to her inadequacy. When we attempt to solve her problem, we fail her. She may be discouraged and faltering but most likely is not helpless and can do for herself if given a chance. Even though our attempts to advise come out of our desire to help, she hears the disguised message behind our advice that criticizes, even invalidates, her decision-making abilities. This likely lowers her self-esteem.

As she tells us her story, if we are caught up in the details and circumstances of it, focused on our own performance and trying to find answers for her, we are not really listening—our mind is elsewhere, and we have failed her in the one area where we could have helped her most.

For personal growth to be real and lasting, it must come from the client's own conviction. Peer counseling is not about finding a solution. It is about sharing of self, experiencing a relationship. Peer counselors who see the client's problematic situation as a natural part of life instead of a disaster and who see her attempts to deal with difficulties as a step in her growth are more likely to give the kind of help that lasts. Fostering strength and self-esteem is the peer counselor's proper focus and is of far more value than finding a solution to the client's immediate problem. Effective peer counselors do *not* give advice.

> If I am who I am because I am who I
>   am, and you are who you are
>   because you are who you are,
>   then I am who I am and you are
>   who you are.
> But if I am who I am because you are
>   who you are, and you are who you
>   are because I am who I am,
>   then I am not I nor are you, you.
>
> Rabbi Menachem Mendel of Kotzk
> [quoted in Raz 1997, p. 73]

And now, with the lesson on not giving advice having been given sufficient attention—or perhaps beaten to death—we are ready for the next lesson.

When to Use Decision-Making Responses

Generally, assisting a client in exploring options and making decisions is not viable until well into the session. Only then can we have enough information to determine whether the client might benefit from such an approach. Before we look at the actual steps of the decision-making process, let us consider the kind of evidence that indicates whether the client is ready to work on decision making.

A client who may benefit from decision-making responses is one who has been an active participant in the counseling session, having freely told her story and having seemingly understood and benefited from our reflection of the content and feelings of what she has said. Her mood is hopeful rather than despairing. She presents herself as being in control of her destiny rather than a victim of circumstances beyond her control. She may give a direct indication of a readiness to explore options and make decisions. She may say, for example, "I am wondering what to do next, what direction to take." Her use of the word "I" is an indication that she may be taking responsibility for her dilemma and for finding a resolution.

A client who is stuck—repeats her story endlessly—may benefit from being approached with a plan for decision making. Chances are we will not get very far in this mode, but it might serve to help her become more aware that her present path is not constructive. It may also serve to let us know whether we should terminate the counseling session. Some repeat callers to crisis lines tell the same story each time they call—sometimes for months or years. (Chapter 9 on "Telephone Counseling" addresses this further.)

Also, attempting a problem-solving approach with a client who never "looks before she leaps" may be productive. This type of client acts without stopping to evaluate the possible results of her actions. She is like the airplane pilot who announces to the passengers the good news, "We are making good time," and the bad news, "We are lost." She seems not to understand why her actions do not work; she may say her actions are "jinxed"—and believe it. Even if she is not receptive to a problem-solving approach, suggesting it may help her become more aware that she is groping in the dark.

The client who asks for our advice probably is not ready to explore options. If she asks what she should do, we can simply respond to the content of what she said: "You are wishing I could give you an answer to your problem," or reflect what she seems to be feeling: "Not knowing the solution is frustrating for you."

The client who suffers from the "yes, but" syndrome—she quickly and consistently finds a reason she cannot possibly act on any prospective solutions—is not ready for decision making. This is also true of the highly emotional client. High emotions block logic.

Fortunately, we do not have to be absolutely certain about the client's readiness for decision making. If the weight of the evidence leans on the side of attempting to explore options and make decisions, we should not wait until the evidence conclusively assures success. This approach has a "fail-safe." We can go back to reflecting content and feelings any time the client shows her inability or unwillingness to proceed with decision making.

A Model for Exploring Options and Making Decisions

It may be helpful for the peer counselor, and the client if she wishes, to make notes while proceeding through the following steps. The client may want to take her own notes with her when she leaves. (In keeping with the confidentiality policy that is honored by agencies that use volunteers, the peer counselor should destroy her own notes in the presence of the client. The peer counselor should never keep notes—other than statistical information the agency may require for funding purposes—and should never give notes to the client, except those of a referral.)

As we go through the steps of the decision-making model, keep in mind that it is appropriate and desirable to intermingle responding to content and responding to feelings. At the end of this chapter is a dialogue between a peer counselor and a client demonstrating how the process works.

Step 1. *Define the problem and ascertain that the client wants to work on it.* Often the reason a client has not worked on her problem is that she does not have a clear picture of what is wrong. You've probably heard the old saying that defining the problem goes 99 percent of the way toward solving it. I believe this to be true.

The client may tend to ramble as she attempts to verbalize her thoughts. As a result, the peer counselor may have trouble pinpointing and summarizing the problem. Sometimes it is helpful to ask the client how she would like her life to be different. This approach helps her focus on her values, and helps the peer counselor obtain a clearer picture of the client's difficulty and how she would like it changed. Even then, rather than cite a specific situation she would like changed, the client will often generalize by saying she wishes to be happier, richer, better liked, or healthier. Responses such as these also adapt themselves to the decision-making steps. If the client is not clear about what her problem is, the peer counselor should not jump to conclusions and put words in her mouth. The agenda must remain the client's. For present purposes, the issue is whatever she states to be her problem. If what she proposes as *the* problem is only a symptom of a bigger problem, the symptom should be treated as the problem. If the client cannot focus well enough to define her problem, return to reflecting content and feelings.

If the client agrees that we have accurately identified and summarized her problem, we should ask whether she would like the two of us to talk about what she might do to resolve it. If she does not wish to do this, there is no point in attempting to encourage her to do so. She may say, "There's nothing I can do about it," or "There's no solution to my problem." In such a case, we should immediately abandon the exploration of options and return to reflecting content and feelings: for example, "You feel it is hopeless to try to do anything about your problem."

If a problem definition is agreed upon, and the focus is on only one problem, proceed to Step 3; if the client defines several problems, proceed to Step 2.

Step 2. *Separate the problems.* Allow the client to select the problem she considers to have the highest priority. Working on more than one problem at a time can be confusing and counterproductive. Encourage the client to set priorities and focus on one problem at a time. Remind the client that, though only one difficulty can be dealt with at a time, others can be addressed later.

Step 3. *Taking the priority problem the client selected, determine what actions, if any, she has already tried.* Often the client has attempted to address her problem. Have her summarize what she has already tried and to what extent these efforts have been effective. If the actions were helpful, ascertain in what ways they were helpful; if not, why not. Encouraging the client to explore solutions she has already tried and found effective may suggest methods she may want to use in the future, and exploring methods she has found not to be effective may reveal avenues to discontinue.

Step 4. *Redefine the problem by summarizing and restating what has been discussed so far.* In the process of exploring, the client may see the problem differently from when she first stated it. We can work with her to redefine it.

Step 5. *Engage the client in brainstorming—come up with possible solutions and avenues of action (include the ones she has already tried that seem to have promise).* We may also offer options, being careful this does not come through as advice. One way to accomplish this is to offer more than one option. This makes clear that we have no agenda but are merely trying to offer a broader context from which to work. It is preferable, however, for the client to put possible options on the table first. With the client, make a mental list of the possible solutions. Assist the client in deciding which of these possibilities appears to her to be the best option to explore. Sometimes a naive client will come up with an option that is contrary to generally accepted, verifiable fact. We can inform her of the facts while making it clear that she has a right to make her own decisions. For example, if the client told us that she had decided to take her blood pressure medication only when she was especially excited, despite her doctor's instructions, we could tell her it is our understanding that blood pressure medication must be taken as prescribed to be effective, and to take it only sporadically could be dangerous.

Step 6. *Determine with the client whether the selected option is within her control.* If not, eliminate this option from the list, go back, and choose another. Proceed until one is chosen that *is* within her control. The client may think changing others will "fix" her problem. It may be helpful to her to consider what control, if any, she has over others. In the process she may realize that she actually has very little, if any, such control. Ideally, this exploration will help her realize she does have control over how she deals with the other person's behavior.

Step 7. *Determine with the client the possible consequences of the selected option.* Consider what price she would have to pay if she took the selected route—and whether she is willing to pay it. Everything has its price. For example, the price the client would pay for change might be discipline and hard work, acquiring new habits, or even adopting a new lifestyle. She might need professional therapy for an extended time, which would require money, time, commitment, and intense emotional involvement. None of these come easily.

In order to make changes in her life, she might have to take risks. Acting differently in a relationship, for example, automatically means an adjustment on the part of the significant other, and he or she might not be willing to do this. The client might have to change jobs, break up with a spouse or friend, or move to another part of the world. She might have to exercise, change diets, lose weight, go back to school, or change careers. She might have to look into her soul and challenge her long-held religious beliefs, look at them in the light of day, and, if they defy her logic, find a spiritual replacement that does not. She might have to do hard things.

For the decision the client makes to be realized, she not only has to make the decision, but must also be willing to pay the price of its activation. If she does not realize and come to terms with the price she will have to pay, her decision making will be in vain and she may feel like a failure. It probably would be better if she deliberately chose to leave the situation as it is. She then can at least know she is living with a choice that is her own.

If she is willing to pay the price for the selected option, go on to Step 8. If not, eliminate the option. Go back to the list, choose another option, and process it through Steps 6 and 7. Taking the options one at a time, determine with the client the possible consequences—what price she would have to pay if she took that route and whether she is willing to pay it.

Step 8. *Process each of the remaining possible solutions through Steps 6 and 7.* Then summarize, naming all the possible options for which she is willing to pay the price. With the client, select the ones that seem to her to represent the best trade-off between the price she has to pay and the potential payoff.

Step 9. *Assist the client in dividing the operations required to activate the proposed solution into small steps.* Goals are sometimes not realized because of the confusion resulting from trying to do too much at once. Success is promoted by separating the action into small steps.

Step 10. *Determine with the client the appropriate time to begin the action.* Sometimes a decision is made with all good intentions of carrying it out—later. For actions to be successful, they must be begun and persistently continued to completion. Work with the client to establish a schedule of action.

Step 11. *Determine with the client how she will know the selected options are working.* Exploring with her how she will know if her new resolution is working will give her clues to watch for as she puts her plans into action. This can prevent her blindly following an unsuccessful course of action and also encourages her to contemplate the results of putting her goals into action. Looking ahead to a triumphant outcome motivates one to begin acting.

Step 12. *Summarize what has occurred so far.* It is easy to get so absorbed in details of exploring options and making decisions that we and the client are distracted from the core issues. Now is the time for the peer counselor to reinforce the plans the client just made by summarizing the goal, the plan of action, and ways of determining whether the plan is working.

As these steps are followed, new possible options may arise at any time. We can simply add them to the list and go back and process them as we did the others. If at any point in exploring options and making decisions she stops her deep involvement, disengage. Keep in mind the goal of peer counseling: *to provide an environment that is conducive to the client's better knowing, accepting, and loving herself.* If the process seems not to be working, we should go back to responding to content and reflecting feelings.

We can further support the client in her plans by inviting her to come back in (or phone again) whenever she wishes.

It is highly improbable that a peer counselor will be able to walk the client through all the decision-making steps in one session. Most clients cannot deal with this much detail at one sitting. Changing, if it happens at all, is slow; the client simply cannot become another person overnight—that would be like jumping out of her skin. Also, in peer counseling sessions or phone calls, time limits probably will prohibit the completion of the steps. If not hurried, exploring these steps makes a lengthy discussion; to hurry would defeat the purpose.

In any event, for those clients with whom it is appropriate, there is a great advantage in beginning the process and going part of the way even if it is not finished. The client can always come back in or phone back to proceed.

An Example of Exploring Options and Making Decisions

You may remember Debra from Chapter 3. Here is an extension of that dialogue demonstrating how to help a client explore options and make decisions. Notice how decision-making responses are intermingled with responses to content and feelings. The process of using these three types of responses can be compared to driving an automobile with a stick shift.

There is an appropriate time to use each gear, and one must be alert to the need for a sudden shifting of gears.

DEBRA: (*With anger*) I'm exhausted. I've had to do laundry every morning this week before I took my children to day care and went to work. And then after work, I have to pick them up, drag them around while I do errands, go home, cook dinner, supervise the children's baths and put them to bed, clean up the kitchen, and get my clothes ready for work the next day. It's that way every week, and do I get any help? Of course not! My husband just sits in front of the TV all the time. Says he's tired! He thinks *he's* tired!

PEER C: You're exhausted and your husband does not help you with the work. (*Responding to content*)

DEBRA: You got it! I don't know how much longer I can keep this up. I've only been working six months, but with the children now, we need the money.

PEER C: You don't know how much longer you can survive this pace, but you need the money. (*Responding to content*)

DEBRA: (*Calmer now*) The worst part is I'm afraid I'm not patient with the children. I mean I have so little time with them anyway. And we used to have a good marriage.

PEER C: You are concerned about your relationship with your children and with your husband. (*Responding to feeling*)

DEBRA: I just feel my whole life changing.

PEER C: Mm-hm. (*By compassionate tone of voice, responding to feeling*)

DEBRA: (*With anger*) After I work hard all day, he wants to have sex. Ha!

PEER C: You're too tired to have sex, and also you resent his not helping you. (*Responding to content and feelings*)

DEBRA: Yes, can't he see how unfair it is?

PEER C: You're feeling angry. (*Responding to feeling*)

DEBRA: Well he did try to help when I first went to work. Said he would clean up the kitchen. Put the dishes in the dishwasher. Big deal! Didn't even wipe off the counter!

For three fifty-minute sessions, Debra talked about her feelings— much of it about how angry she was at her husband. The peer counselor listened, responding to the content of what she said and reflecting her feelings. Debra seemed to use this support productively to get in touch with her feelings. At the fourth session, she began by saying:

DEBRA: You know, I seem to be going around in circles. It feels good to be able to tell you about my situation—real good! I'm beginning to see that anybody would feel stressed out in my situation.

PEER C: You're saying being stressed out is normal in your situation. (*Responding to content*)

DEBRA: Yes. I mean even a superwoman wouldn't be able to do what I'm trying to do and do it well. I've been confiding in my friends about how stressed I am, and they admit they are also—though some of them don't value good housekeeping as much as I do. But this doesn't change anything except that I don't feel so negative toward myself. I'm still angry with Dave. But that doesn't change anything either. I want my situation to change.

PEER C: Debra, as we've talked over the past few weeks, what I understand you to be saying is that you want four things: a life where you don't feel so stressed, more time with the children, your husband to help you with the housework, and your relationship with him to improve. In thinking how you want your life to be different, does that about sum it up? (*Step 1*)

DEBRA: It sure does.

PEER C: Would you like us to work together on some possible solutions you might pursue to change your situation? (*Step 1*)

DEBRA: I sure would. I'm willing to do almost anything to improve things. I know if they keep on going as they are, my health is going to suffer. And they are sure not going to change unless I do something different. But you know, when you were repeating what I had said my problem was, I realized my biggest problem is that I feel my marriage deteriorating. I mean we used to talk, and now we don't even have time to talk and, if we do, I'm too angry.

PEER C: You're saying that, though all the things we have talked about are problems, your relationship with Dave is your number one difficulty. (*In this case the client has taken care of Step 2,*

"Separate the problems." The peer counselor is merely reinforcing the definition by restating it.)

DEBRA: Yes. I guess nothing else can change until that changes.

PEER C: For now, then, since we can work on only one thing at a time, let's work on what you might do to improve your relationship with your husband. (*Step 2*) It might be helpful for us to take a look at what you have done so far, if anything, to improve your relationship with Dave. (*Step 3*)

DEBRA: Absolutely nothing. I've been so stressed out I've only been focusing on getting my work done. I guess I've done lots of things to make our relationship worse. I find this hard to believe, but I'm just now realizing that's my main problem. If we got along, and I was not so resentful, I might be able to think about what else I could do to get out from under some of this stress.

PEER C: You're saying you are just now realizing that your relationship with your husband is your main problem and contributes greatly toward your stress. Also, you're saying you haven't tried anything to better your relationship. You did mention in an earlier session that you had asked him to help with the housework, but that he just watched TV and didn't help you. (*Step 3 and 4*)

DEBRA: Yeah, that idea sure didn't get off the ground.

PEER C: Do you have any idea why he didn't respond to your request? (*Step 3*)

DEBRA: Well, it wasn't exactly a request—it was more like a command, and that's probably why it didn't work.

PEER C: Okay. Let's begin by pretending we have a blackboard here and we'll put on it: "Ways to improve relationship with hus-

band." Why don't we begin by just brainstorming? Just saying whatever comes to mind. What can you think of that you
might do to improve your relationship with Dave? (*Step 5*)

DEBRA: Well, let's see. Hm. Maybe if we went out together more
often. My sister and I sometimes swap baby sitting.

PEER C: You're saying it might improve your relationship for the
two of you to spend some pleasant times together. Can you
think of anything else we should list on our make-believe
blackboard? (*Step 5*)

DEBRA: Well, it's obvious that Dave and I are going to have to communicate some way—to understand what goes on with the
other—but I've tried to talk to him. Well, I guess I've tried to
tell him what's going on with me. I always feel so rushed—
and the children running around screaming.

PEER C: So you believe it's of utmost importance that you and Dave
communicate with each other, but so far you haven't been in
a position to do so. Have you thought of the two of you going
to a professional therapist? (*Step 5*)

DEBRA: In fact, I have. But we really can't afford it since our insurance won't pay.

PEER C: Let's see, working with a professional therapist is not an
option for you, but you really do wish to communicate well
with him. What else can you think of that you could do to
improve communications? (*Step 5*)

DEBRA: I just can't think of anything else. Can you?

PEER C: I wonder what the possibilities are that you and he might
go on a little vacation together—just the two of you. (*Step 5*)

DEBRA: It would be hard to do, but that sure would get his attention. He says I never want to go anywhere or do anything.

PEER C: Another idea that came to me—since your housework takes a great deal of your time and energy—I wonder if hiring a housecleaning service would relieve you of some of the time-related stress, giving you more time to be with Dave. (*Step 5*)

DEBRA: Do you know how much those things cost? I might as well quit my job and stay home and do it myself!

PEER C: So that's out. Let's stop a minute here and see where we are in this brainstorming. That leaves one, the two of you going out at night more, and two, the two of you trying to get away for a short vacation. Can you think of anything else? (*Step 5*)

DEBRA: Well, our sex life is terrible. I guess I could try to make more time for that, but it's difficult to have sex with someone you don't like. While I really do believe I still love him, I don't like him right now.

PEER C: Sounds like you're saying the relationship will have to improve before you can feel close enough to him to be physically intimate. (*Responding to content*)

DEBRA: That's true. Right now it just causes me to dislike him more. But that's a real problem, because when I refuse, he gets even more distant from me. I know I'm driving him away. But can't he understand I don't want sex with him when we're not close in other ways? (*Begins crying*)

PEER C: (*Allows a short silence, then, with an empathic tone*) It really hurts when he doesn't understand. And your unsatisfactory sexual relations is not only the result but becomes part of the cause of your alienation from each other. (*Responding to feeling and content*)

DEBRA: (*Ceases crying*) Yes! Well, that's not how our trouble started. We once had a very good sex life. We can again if other things get worked out. I'm just not going to worry about that. Worrying about it won't help and I need to concentrate on what I can do to help us.

PEER C: To review, so far we have come up two possibilities. One, the two of you going out at night more, and two, the two of you trying to get away for a short vacation. Can you think of anything else? (*Step 5*)

DEBRA: That's all I can think of.

PEER C: Okay. Let's take just one of these options and explore it in greater detail. Which one would you like us to start with? (*Step 5*)

DEBRA: Why don't we take the first one first.

PEER C: Okay. This is that you two might go out more at night. It's always good to determine to what extent the action we want to take is within our control. Do you think Dave will agree to this? (*Step 6*)

DEBRA: Oh, yes. He would love it. But, you know, I think I would resent the time it took and just be angry with him. And we would just go to a movie or something. We still couldn't talk. I think this may not be a good thing to try.

PEER C: Okay, then, that leaves the possibility of you two taking a vacation together. How do you think Dave will feel about this? (*Step 6*)

DEBRA: I believe he'll agree to it. He's complained that we never do anything.

PEER C: It sounds like you think approaching him about the possibility of the two of you taking a vacation is the way to begin. Sometimes it helps to anticipate the obstacles and plan ahead of time how you will deal with them. Let's look ahead a bit and imagine what obstacles, if any, you're likely to encounter in approaching him. (*Step 7*)

DEBRA: I would sure hate for him to think we were going away for fun, and then, after we get there, hit him with this. Maybe I could tell him ahead of time that I'm concerned about our relationship, and we need to work on it—and that I'm willing to do my part. I think he's worried about our relationship too, and now I see more clearly that I've not listened to his side at all—I've just complained. If I tell him ahead of time why I want us to go, and tell him I'm willing to listen to his side, I believe he'll welcome it. But then again, he might not.

PEER C: You're saying, if you approach him with honesty and on a positive note, you believe he will agree to go, but also that there is a possibility you will get your hopes up only to have them shattered. (*Step 7*)

DEBRA: Well, I'm willing to take that chance. I've got to start somewhere.

PEER C: If he agrees to go, what about the practical aspects of the trip? What do you think you will run into there? (*Step 7*)

DEBRA: Well, we both like camping, so it won't cost much. And we both have a few vacation days coming up. The biggest problem will be getting a sitter. But I believe my sister will do that.

PEER C: When will you ask Dave? (*Step 10*)

DEBRA: I'll pick a time when he's not frustrated about work—I can tell. Yes, I think I'll do it next week.

Peer C: After you get to your camping spot and have told him of your concerns, how do you think you'll know if your plan is working? (*Step 11*)

DEBRA: I'll try my best not to be on the defensive. And if he tells me how he feels, I'll know his intentions at least. And if we can go so far as to decide how he can help to relieve me of some of the time pressures, I think we have a good chance.

PEER C: And after you get home, in the days to follow, how do you think you'll know if your plan is working? (*Step 11*)

DEBRA: I'll have to see him in action when we get home to know if my plan worked. I think I'm ready to find out where he stands. If he's not with me in rearing the children and being interested in my health, I'll just go from there. But you know, I believe if I approach him with a good attitude—without being angry—well, I believe he does love me. I think I've wanted to be in control of the children and the housework. I may just have to think of it as our being partners and let him choose which part of the work he prefers—I may not get things done as I would like—that will be hard. But not as hard as what I put up with now.

PEER C: You've concluded that there's a good chance you can work things out with Dave. You feel optimistic. But even if it doesn't work out, you'll have more data with which to plan your future. (*Step 12*)

DEBRA: Yes.

5

Beginning a Peer Counseling Session

Preparing Ourselves

As I travel to my volunteer work, I have found it helpful to prepare myself mentally by taking stock of my emotions. And once I
arrive at work and approach the entrance of the building, I do my
best to leave my personal baggage on the doorstep. So far, in my
many years of doing volunteer work, my personal baggage, though
admittedly somewhat lightened, has never failed to be waiting faith-
fully for me when I leave.

The peer counselor should make it a point to arrive at the
counseling location fifteen minutes or so before the changing of
the shift to allow time for briefing on any pertinent happenings at
the agency, checking the appointment book, and assembling any
needed supplies. Also, for face-to-face counseling, the counseling
room may need to be prepared. Most peer counseling rooms are
also used for groups and may need rearranging to accommodate
working with an individual. This involves placing two chairs opposite each other in one corner of the room, at comfortable angles,
close enough to allow intimacy but not so close as to cause inva-
sion of each other's space. If one of the chairs is higher than the
other, the peer counselor should use the lower one to avoid a
teacher–student type of atmosphere. A clock is an absolute necessity. It should be placed so that the peer counselor, without being
obvious, can glance at it occasionally so as to be aware of how much
session time remains. (Depending on a watch does not work well

for obvious reasons.) Placing a box of tissues where the client can comfortably reach them is a thoughtful gesture. The room will be more conducive to intense concentration if the drapes, or lamps, are prepared so the light is neither dim nor glaring.

First-Time Jitters

Most new peer counselors are nervous before beginning their first session or taking their first phone call. This is natural and is more likely an emotional response to his or her concern and commitment than an indication of incompetence. Consider how the noted psychologist Carl Rogers approached a therapeutic encounter:

> There is something I do before I start a session. I let myself know that I am enough. Not perfect. Perfect wouldn't be enough. But that I am human, and that is enough. There is nothing this man can say or do or feel that I can't feel in myself. I can be with him. I am enough. [Cited in Kushner 1996, p. 7]

About Socializing

When they first arrive (or first phone), many clients sound cheerful and gregarious. Like most of us, they have learned to put on a happy face when going out into the world of people. When I first began peer counseling, I found myself responding in kind to the client's sociability. This often led to spending so much time socializing that a "coming-down" time was necessary and the client had a difficult time switching to the actual counseling session. I soon came to accept that the counseling session is not the place for socializing. This does not, of course, mean the peer counselor must use a gloom-and-doom approach. (This might lead to the client's attempting to counsel the peer counselor.) We can be friendly and caring and still maintain a soberness and respect for the client's situation. We can recognize that, however on top of the world the client may seem to be, something is going on that caused him to seek counseling. I have seen clients, upon entering the counseling session, switch unbelievably quickly from a cheerful facade to tears. We must remember that this is the client's day, his time for us to be attentive. And it is up to us to get things started in a way that is conducive to his talking about his concerns.

Once seated, in face-to-face counseling, it is up to the peer counselor to replace socializing with silence and a look of expectancy, making it easier for the client to begin. At this point some peer counselors utter a simple "okay" (using a tone that indicates, "Now we're settled and it's okay for you to begin"). In telephone counseling, after responding briefly to whatever social formality the client may initiate, the peer counselor must become silent, allowing the session to begin.

Who Talks First?

Assuming any perfunctory socializing has ceased, who talks first? How a session begins is of great importance. It sets the tone for the entire session or series of sessions. The client often has difficulty in beginning to talk about his concerns—it's not easy to share innermost thoughts and feelings with a stranger. However, whoever begins talking is the one likely to take responsibility for the session.

Peer counselors are often inclined to take the lead at the beginning of a session. Telephone counselors often begin by saying, "I'm glad you called," or "How can I help?" Face-to-face counselors often ask, "What brings you here today?" At first glance, statements such as these seem natural, easy, friendly, and caring. Unfortunately, they also practically ensure that the client will expect the peer counselor to take responsibility for the session. The client is often only too eager for the peer counselor to take the lead, and our natural reaction may be to make him comfortable, just as one would a guest. Peer counseling is a different dance; the client leads, the peer counselor follows. The client did not come in or phone to be comfortable, he came in to work. Delving into emotional pain is not a comfortable procedure. We will make it as easy for him as we can without getting in his way, but it is his ball game. In order for the client to benefit from the session and for our volunteer time to be put to the use for which it was intended, he must tell his story. If the client speaks first, he will probably tell his version of his story the way he wishes. If he merely responds to our statements, he will be telling our version of his story, which will result in both the peer counselor and the client working somewhat in the dark.

After the volunteer has responded a few times to the content of the client's story, the client will have a wealth of information about what the counseling session is going to be like. He will know that, though he is expected to do the talking, the peer counselor is listening, *really* listening, listening so well, in fact, that she or he can paraphrase what he just said. He will know that the counselor is not putting a moral judgment on anything he says, that it is all right to say anything he wishes—even to change his mind about what he said earlier. He will know that he is not going to be lectured or given advice, that he cannot expect any answers or quick fixes. He will know that, because the peer counselor has volunteered time to listen, he is in the presence of a caring, patient person. All this knowledge, this permission to explore his dilemma in any way he wishes, makes the difficulty of his taking responsibility for the session worth his work.

Pacing Ourselves

At the start of the counseling session, we do not reflect feelings or assist the client in exploring options or making decisions. We listen and respond to content. We should begin by speaking slowly and calmly. Speaking rapidly can cause the client to feel intimidated and rushed. As the session proceeds and the pace at which the client speaks becomes clear, it is helpful for us to pace our speech to roughly match his.

The Overly Friendly Client

Sometimes, after the perfunctory opening remarks, the client continues to socialize. Since this may be his way of getting into his story, we should give him a little time. However, our responses to his social overtures, though friendly, should be brief and sober. Perhaps this will clue him to begin talking about his concern. If he still continues to socialize—if, for example, he says, "The leaves sure are beautiful this time of year. Last year they were not this beautiful—something about how much rain we've had seems to affect their color," we might say, "You seem to be having trouble getting to what you came in to talk about." Almost invariably the client will say, "Yes, it's hard to talk about it" (and then will tell his story).

But what if the client continues to socialize after this initial confrontation by the peer counselor? It could be that he came in at the suggestion, or demand, of a third party. We can check this out: "Correct me if I'm wrong, but I'm feeling you don't really wish to be here (or to have phoned us)." At this point most clients who were sent in by someone else will admit that counseling really was not their idea. The peer counselor then may respond: "We can work together only if *you* wish to do so. Why don't we call it quits for now. You may make an appointment to come back (or may phone us again) any time you wish."

Usually this will resolve the impasse, with the client either deciding on the spot that he does want to work on his concern or on his terminating the session.

But what if the client insists that he came to the session of his own accord but continues, for no apparent reason, to attempt to socialize? In peer counseling there are times when risk taking is appropriate, and this may be one of those times. The client may be socializing simply because he is lonely. (This is often the case with clients who telephone.) He may not even have identified his trouble as loneliness. The peer counselor can explore with the client whether or not loneliness is his major difficulty: "Since you haven't mentioned any particular difficulty you are having right now, I am wondering if you might be lonely." The client will probably be relieved to have identified his emptiness as loneliness. Only then is he in a position to explore ways to fill this need. He might talk at length about how difficult it is for him to get with people, and with his objective clarified, he might be willing to take on the difficult task of reaching out to people.

While our helping the client identify and label his concern can be extremely helpful to him, we are not expected to have solutions to his loneliness. And our job certainly does not involve any attempt to combat his loneliness by offering our companionship, though we might offer a referral to a social club whose activities are in his area of interest. (See Chapter 8 for more about referring.) Usually, though, the client comes in or phones about a specific difficulty and he socializes either because he dreads talking about it or does not know how to begin.

Here is an example of how we might begin a session with an overly friendly client.

Carl has an appointment with a peer counselor at a Men's Center. Upon arriving, he walks up to the desk and says:

CARL: Hi! How are you today?

PEER C: Fine, how are you?

CARL: I have an appointment with Ed.

PEER C: I'm Ed. I'm glad to meet you, Carl. We'll just walk this way where we'll have more privacy. (*As the two men walk down the hall to the peer counseling room, Carl continues talking.*)

CARL: This is a great day, don't you think? I went for a run this morning. The air was so fresh and crisp. It just makes one feel great. I can run seven miles now. I think that's pretty good, don't you?

PEER C: Yes, it is. (*Carl continues talking as he spontaneously takes a seat and tilts his chair on its two back legs.*)

CARL: I started running about two years ago. Before that I wasn't in shape at all. My friend, who lives in California, came to visit me two years ago and he was in great shape. I asked him how he kept in such great shape and he said he ran every day so I decided to do the same. Are you into running?

PEER C: Carl, correct me if I'm wrong, but I suspect you did not come in to talk about running.

CARL: (*Hanging head*) Well, yes. You're right. I guess I think if I act happy I'll be happy. You see, I lost my job last week, we don't have any savings, and I am so upset I can't eat or sleep.

Silences in the Beginning of the Session

Although rare, an occasional client will begin the session in complete silence. In face-to-face and telephone counseling, the peer counselor remains silent to allow the client to begin. One advantage of face-to-face counseling is that the peer counselor's attentive body posture and facial expression of expectancy is an invitation for the client to begin. On the telephone, if neither the client nor the peer counselor is speaking, neither can be sure the other is there. Thus the wait can be longer when face to face than when on the phone. In either case, although the wait is only a few seconds, it can seem much longer to the peer counselor.

After a few seconds, if the client does not begin talking, some peer counselors choose to say, "I'll just wait until you are ready," and do so by sitting in silence with the client (or waiting in silence on the phone). Other peer counselors, myself included, would feel uncomfortable with a long silence. Examples of things a peer counselor can say to break the silence and still leave the responsibility for the session with the client are:

> "Sometimes it's hard to begin."
> "Sometimes it's difficult to share your feelings with a stranger."
> "Sometimes an easy place to begin is to talk about what prompted you to phone (or come in)."

If one of these statements brings no response, breaking our own rule by using a more directive response, "Start anywhere you like," will often do the trick. If none of these invitations brings a response, a good guess is that the client either came in against his wishes or is deeply depressed.

If the client came in at the request of a third party and does not really wish to talk with the counselor (and if he reveals this information), the peer counselor can explain (as noted earlier in this chapter) that they can work together only when he wishes to work, and that he is welcome to come back (or phone) any time he wishes. If the client is not willing to reveal his reason for seeking peer counseling, dragging it out of him serves no purpose.

Some clients are deeply depressed, causing them to be silent and unresponsive or unable to talk for crying. Some indications of depression are drooped shoulders, hanging head, unresponsiveness, and profuse tears. If none of the foregoing statements elicit a response from the client, the counselor might suggest that he appears depressed. At this point we might tell the client that peer counselors are not qualified to treat depression but that in many cases it is very treatable, and then ask him if he would like a referral. (Chapter 10 addresses depression and Chapter 8 addresses giving referrals.)

Here is an example of how a peer counselor might begin a session with a client who is hesitant to talk. The client and peer counselor have just entered the counseling room and found their seats.

PEER C: Okay.

DAVE: (*Silence*)

PEER C: (*Silent for about twenty seconds, then speaks slowly in order to set the pace for a slow-moving conversation*) Sometimes it's hard to get started.

DAVE: (*After about five seconds*) Yes.

PEER C: (*After about ten seconds*) Sometimes an easy place to begin is to go back to what you were thinking when you made the appointment.

DAVE: (*After about five seconds*) I was very upset then. And I'm still upset.

PEER C: (*After waiting about ten seconds*) You were upset when you made the appointment and you're still upset.

DAVE: That's right. My doctor called with my test results, and my whole world is turned upside down.

PEER C: (*After waiting another five or ten seconds*) Learning your test results has changed your whole world.

DAVE: Yes. I always thought I was pretty healthy. I never thought I would ever be really sick. I don't know what I'm going to do. I don't know how I'm going to handle this.

One-Liners

Let us assume that, in the beginning of the session, the peer counselor has managed an effective silence that allows the client to take responsibility for the session. Some clients, though willing to talk, begin with a single bumper-sticker-size statement such as "I don't know what to do," or "I have a problem," and then wait for the peer counselor to speak. For many of us, our automatic response to anyone who says, "I have a problem," is "What is it?"

A better response is to respond to the content by saying the client's words back to him: "You have a problem," or "You don't know what to do." After such a response the client will usually elaborate on his concerns.

Another one-liner that clients often use: "I don't quite know where to begin." Responding to this statement in a nondirective way can be a bit tricky. The first response that new peer counselors usually think of is, "Start anywhere you like." At first glance it may seem that this is a good response, but actually it is a suggestion, advice, directive counseling, a lead. A better response is, "It's hard for you to know just where to start." This latter statement responds to the content by paraphrasing the client's statement, playing it back to him, demonstrating to him he was heard, and following along behind. It is nondirective counseling.

I know that drawing this fine line between nondirective and directive responses may seem persnickety, but the difference is that a precedent is set for the entire session concerning whether the counselor leads or follows the client. I learned this the hard way by spending entire sessions trying to undo my original, leading remarks. And many times I have heard a peer counselor at the beginning of a phone conversation respond by taking the lead, though ever so slightly. Invariably he or she does most of the talking, and ends the call frustrated that the client did not talk very much.

Hesitancy may be the client's normal way of communicating. He may not value himself very highly or ever have had a good listener, or he may just be a private person by nature. He may be quite comfortable with his limited inputs. If we follow along, giving one-sentence reflections to his one-sentence statements, or, after a time, putting his statements together and summarizing them for him, he may realize he is in a safe place and expand his talking time.

A client's refusal to talk, or hesitancy, is rare. It is addressed here to prepare you to handle the situation if you encounter it. In general, a client's reason for seeking peer counseling wins out over his dread of beginning to talk and compels him to tell his story.

The Nonstop Talker

More common than the individual who continues socializing, remains silent, or utters one-liners is the client who jumps right into his problem, making it difficult for us to get a word in edgewise. But we must. In the beginning of each session we need to set a pattern of the client's telling his story and our reflecting it back to him. With a nonstop talker, however, we find no neat breaks that allow us to respond (as happened in practice role plays during training). The client just goes on and on, continuing without pause until he has gotten far into his story and set a pattern that will continue well into the session unless we interrupt. If the nonstop talker does not pause to breathe after a few minutes—at most— we need to break into the monologue and change it into a dialogue. In the beginning of a session, if the only way we can speak is to interrupt, then interrupt we must. We can forget momentarily what mother taught us about not interrupting. Our client will not lose his train of thought if we have listened well and respond accurately to the content of what he said. Quite the contrary, he will, by hearing our summary of what he said, be better able to go forward in an organized way. The client needs to know we are there and that we heard.

It is surprisingly easy for a peer counselor to wait too long in the beginning of the session to begin responding. If we hear our client rambling along as he gazes at the ceiling, using phrases erratic and disjointed, possibly repeating himself, it could be that we have not reminded him we are there.

Jumping in is hard to do, especially with a nonstop talker, but we must do so if he is to benefit from our being his sounding board. The interrupting should be done in a matter-of-fact rather than an apologetic way.

"Let me stop you a minute and see if I'm with you. You are saying . . ."
or
"Wait. Let me be sure I am hearing you correctly. It sounds like . . ."

Phrases such as these will invariably bring him back to the present and help him realize he is actually being listened to. He may sigh, slow down, and begin telling it more like it is.

Here is an example of how we might begin a session with a client who is a non-stop talker. Mark arrives early for his appointment at the center. The peer counselor at the desk greets him and shows him to the waiting room. Shortly after, another peer counselor, Ron, goes out to greet Mark.

PEER C: Hi. I'm Ron. Just come on back, Mark. (*He leads the way to the counseling room. They are seated. Mark begins right away.*)

MARK: It's my job. I think my boss is trying to get rid of me. I've worked there fourteen years and lately everything has changed. First, all those new, young workers were hired. Then my boss started giving my projects to them. I was doing them just like I always did. I do a good job. But he took them away from me and gave me little boring jobs. The time at work seems so long. I know he's just trying to get me to quit and he may just manage it if he keeps treating me like this, but I can't get unemployment if I quit. He's just trying to get me to quit instead of firing me and I know . . .

PEER C: Mark, let me stop you a minute to see if I'm with you. You're saying that, after fourteen years of doing a good job for your company, your boss is suddenly treating you differently. He's giving projects you normally would get to new and younger workers. You think he's trying to get you to quit so he won't be faced with firing you.

MARK: That's right. I'm really worried and I don't know what to do.

A client who is accustomed to speaking for a long time without pausing may continue to do this throughout the session. It may be necessary for us to interrupt several times by saying, for example,

"Wait a minute. Let's see where we are now . . ."
or
"Before you go on, let's look at what you've said up until now . . ."
or
"Just a minute, Mark. Let me play back what you have said."

The client generally accepts these interruptions without question. It is important that we show no aggravation or impatience at the client's long speeches. Our not allowing the long speeches without interruption at the beginning of the session help to alert the client that we play a nondirective but active role in the session. Sometimes, after the first few interruptions, the client will pause after a statement to wait for us to acknowledge his words.

The Average Talker

We have addressed how to handle clients who are silent or hesitant to talk and clients who are nonstop talkers; fortunately, the majority of clients do not fall into either of these categories. Most clients begin talking at a natural pace; that is, neither holding back nor ranting endlessly. With these more typical talkers, we simply begin, after their initial speech, by responding to the content of what they said. This, actually, is our goal with any client at the beginning of a session, but with the average talker it is much easier to do.

Here is an example of how a peer counselor might begin a session with a more-typical client. Tim phones a crisis line:

PEER C: Hello, this is the crisis line.

TIM: I need to talk to somebody about a problem I'm having. Are you the right person?

PEER C: Yes, I am.

TIM: Well, you see, I'm calling because I don't know what to do. My problem is a rather delicate one and I just need someone to talk with.

PEER C: Mm-hm.

TIM: I've been doing some things that my wife didn't know about. And last night she caught me.

PEER C: Your wife caught you last night.

TIM: That's right. You see, I like to dress up in women's clothes. I don't go out anywhere with them on, you see. It's just something I like to do. It's harmless, but my wife doesn't understand at all. She cried and cried and said she was going to leave me. I don't want to hurt her and I don't want her to leave, but I don't think I can give up dressing up.

PEER C: To you your dressing up is harmless but your wife doesn't understand and is threatening to leave you.

Other Start-up Business

If we have met with the client several times and this is to be the final session of a series, we should remind the client early in the session that this is the last time we will meet together, and we should review what has happened in the previous sessions. This may ease the leave-taking for both client and counselor and also serve to invite closure of the issues discussed previously.

Introduction to Assessing Needs

Assessing the needs of a client is discussed in detail in Chapter 8; however, since it has an impact on the successful beginning of a session, an introduction to the subject may be helpful here. The very beginning of a session, especially a telephone session, is when we assess a client's needs—whether the client needs peer counseling, a referral, to have a present emergency dealt with, or all three. If, for example, we realize his situation may be an emergency, we must switch immediately to emergency mode. (Handling emergency situations is covered in detail in Chapter 10.) If ours is an agency that serves clients face to face, and we establish that the telephone client's need is for peer counseling, our priority goal is to make an appointment for him to come in. Or, if it is obvious the client needs a referral, this has priority. (More about making referrals is provided in Chapter 8.) Making an appointment for the client or giving him a referral as soon as we realize his need may seem like cutting the client off too early in the telephone session, but often he hangs up unexpectedly. For example, when someone whom he does not wish to hear his conversation comes into the room where he is talking, he may just hang up the phone. Before giving a referral or making an appointment, the peer counselor can say, for example:

> "We certainly can talk further about your situation, but before we do it might be advisable for us to make an appointment for you to come to the center so we can talk together without distractions. Our agency offers fifty-minute sessions. You would be talking with me, if you wish, and you can come in more than once. Would you like to make an appointment before we continue talking?"

If the client makes an appointment, care should be taken to give him directions to the center. After taking care of the above priorities, we could continue:

"We can talk a little further right now, if you wish. You were saying . . ."

Since assessing needs is generally done on the telephone when the client first contacts the agency, we do not have that job to do when we walk into a counseling room with a client. But there are exceptions. Sometimes the person the client talked with on the telephone did not assess the client's needs accurately. (Possibly the client did not reveal his needs at the time.) Or maybe the client's needs have changed since that initial contact. In any case, at the beginning of the session the peer counselor needs to keep a third ear open in case peer counseling should prove not to be the priority need at the moment. If the counselor suspects the priority need may be other than peer counseling, he or she can check it out with the client.

If the client in a face-to-face session needs both peer counseling and a referral, it is generally better to wait until the end of the session to give him the referral. During the session, however, the counselor could tell him that he or she will give him the referral when they finish.

Summing Up

In the beginning of the session we want to build the client's confidence and trust in us, the session, and himself by allowing him to take the lead. Our job is to respond to the content of what he says. We want to be especially accurate, so we must listen well. And we need to involve ourselves in the session from the very start so we will not wait long to respond to content. As the client talks, we will be alert to needs he might have other than for peer counseling, but our focus will be on listening and responding to content. Executing a successful beginning of the session requires practice, but quite soon becomes second nature.

It takes courage for a person to seek peer counseling. Our being involved from the onset of the session builds rapport and the client's trust and gets the entire session off to a productive start.

6

Ending a Peer Counseling Session

How Long Should a Peer Counseling Session Last?

A face-to-face counseling session normally lasts fifty minutes and should never be extended beyond this time (except, possibly, for an emergency). Peer counseling is intense work for the client and for the peer counselor; fifty minutes is as long as either can work in the intense manner required of a constructive session. By the end of this period the client has as much new data to take with her as she can effectively work on. Chances are that anything that happens after fifty minutes will be a repeat of what has already transpired. Attempting to prolong the session tends to undermine the effectiveness of what has been accomplished, but it is not written in stone that the session must last the entire fifty minutes.

Telephone sessions vary in length but ordinarily should not run past thirty minutes and should never (except, possibly, in an emergency) run over fifty minutes. It is harder to do intense work by phone. Communications are less complete as the client and peer counselor are unable to see each other, and distractions are likely on both ends. In addition, the agency has a commitment to open the line to other callers after a reasonable length of time. The client can call back, although she might get a different peer counselor the next time. Volunteer agencies do not claim to offer the level of in-depth counseling that requires continuity. If the client's need is for in-depth therapy, a referral to a therapist or to the community mental health agency is in order.

Both face-to-face and telephone sessions should be terminated when the peer counselor judges that the client is no longer benefiting from the session. The basis for judgment is the extent to which the goal of peer counseling is being met; if the client is no longer making progress toward "better knowing, accepting, and loving herself," continuing the session would be counterproductive. If the client avoids working on issues by continuing to socialize, shows evidence of impaired thinking, seems tired and overwhelmed with new thoughts and feelings, or goes over the same material repeatedly, she is not utilizing the counselor's support.

A word of caution, though, concerning the last of the above examples: the client may need to tell her story over and over. Repeating it may be her way of working on her difficulties. She may have experienced a recent shock and is still trying to believe what has occurred. Often such a client will say, "I just can't believe it!" Identifying this scenario is fairly simple, and a client experiencing this transition should be allowed considerable latitude to handle her difficulty in her own way. Other clients, however, repeat themselves because they cannot or will not move beyond their difficulty to understand themselves better and search for ways to cope. In such instances the conversation will seem to drag, going nowhere, making no progress. Such a session should be terminated after a reasonable time. Rome was not built in a day. There will be other times for her to phone or come in, other places where she can get help.

It is difficult to set formal guidelines concerning when a session should be terminated, but in an actual peer counseling session it is not difficult to recognize. Our intuition seems to be a dependable guide, and if we learn well the how-to's of ending a session, we will be able to heed our intuition.

Trainees sometimes assume that a session cannot end until they have practiced their skill of helping the client explore options and make decisions (as discussed in Chapter 4). Actually, there is no direct connection between this skill and the ending of a session. If the skill were being used at the end of the session, it would be a coincidence. It is more likely the peer counselor will be listening and responding to the content of what the client says and observing and reflecting feelings as the session ends. There is no direct connection between ending the session and any of the three basic skills.

The Importance of Ending the Session on Time

Often the client does not want the session to end. She may have found the peer counselor to be the first person in a long time, if ever, who has really listened to and been supportive of her. It may be hard for her to let go and lose the support.

And the counselor may be reluctant to end the session, allowing it to run past the allotted time because he or she simply does not know how to bring about a graceful closure with a persistent client. A more common cause, however, is that the peer counselor is tempted to fantasize that continuing just a few more minutes after the allotted time will contribute greatly toward the client's solving her problem. It will not. Chances are, the entirety of the client's life experiences contributes to the difficulty she is now experiencing, so you can be sure it will not be resolved in fifty minutes. The most that can be accomplished in a few peer counseling sessions is that the client will feel more valued—not a trivial outcome—and that she make a start toward defining her difficulty and learning a process for working on it. Dragging out the session a few minutes after the scheduled ending time will more likely take away from the benefits than add to them. And—if another reason is needed—the peer counselor may have another appointment immediately after the present one, or be needed at the desk.

So the client, and at times the peer counselor, may be disinclined to end the session on time. In most cases, if it were left to the client, I am not sure it would ever end. But end it must. And seeing that it does is the responsibility of the peer counselor.

When to Begin the Ending

When closing a session, the objective is to give some sense of completion to the discussion and to bring both client and peer counselor back to the reality of the remainder of the day. This takes time. Experience will tell when to begin closing—it will differ from client to client—but an average closing time is about five minutes.

If the closing begins too soon, the client may feel cheated, the time will begin to drag, and both parties may be tempted to raise new issues. If the closing is prolonged until the last minute, the client may feel pushed out and the peer counselor may have a sense of leaving things with loose ends dangling.

Closing the session might be compared to landing a plane. Preparations for the landing must be made ahead of time to ensure that the plane comes down slowly and smoothly, avoiding an ear-popping descent and an abrupt halt. However, prolonged endings—circling the runway—serve no useful purpose and are to be avoided.

How to End a Peer Counseling Session

However long or short the session, and no matter why we decide to terminate it, when the clock or our intuition says to end it, we should immediately begin switching from nondirective to directive counseling, to take charge. To continue using the skills of responding to content or reflecting feelings would, as they are designed to do, encourage the client to continue talking. Changing from following the client to leading her is a substantial transition. Most new peer counselors find it difficult to switch into an assertive mode; however, they also find that practice and being taken advantage of by a client a few times make great teachers.

We must pick an appropriate point in the session to begin ending the session. This point should be immediately after we have responded to a statement from the client. This way, we will be interrupting ourselves, not the client. The latter would tend to leave the client's last statement dangling and lead her to suspect that we are so vested in closing the session that we did not hear the last thing said. Below is an example of responding to the client and then closing the session.

KAY: And so, right now, it doesn't look like Adam and I are going to make it together. I don't know how I'm going to get him out of my apartment without a fight. But it may come to that. But as I said, before I do anything big, I want to see how he does on the rehab program.

PEER C: You're not optimistic right now, but you want to try a bit longer. (*Short pause*) Well, our fifty minutes for today are about up. We can meet together for up to four more times if you wish. We covered several issues today that you may want to explore further. Before we go, is there anything more you wish to say about what we have talked about up to this point?

KAY: I guess not. I dread going back to work, and especially back home. I think I'm getting a better handle on some of my difficulties, but I think I still have a long way to go. Things are so hard for me right now. And when I think of the future, it seems overwhelming. But I guess I just need to take one day at a time.

PEER C: I admire your strength and your courage. Would you like to come in the same time next week?

KAY: Yes, this is the best time for me. And, uh, I really appreciate your listening. I'm so tired right now, but I'm glad I have these other visits to work on some of my stuff.

PEER C: Thank you. I'll look forward to seeing you next week. Let's go to the front desk and I'll mark your appointment in the book.

Notice that the peer counselor worked into the ending of the session the information that fifty minutes is allowed for the session and also the number of times they can meet. This is a good way to make sure the client experiences no surprises concerning the sessions. If this information had been offered earlier in the session, it probably would have gotten in the way of the free flow of conversation and caused the client to feel the structure was more important to the peer counselor than her story.

Other examples of peer counselor ending statements are:

"We have talked about a great many things. Perhaps it would be helpful, after you have had time to think about what we talked about today, if we talk again."

"You have a lot to think about. I'm glad you came."

"It seems we have gone as far as we can for this time."

"How about we call it quits for now? We've had a good conversation."

"Before we call it a day, let's see where we are . . ."

"I can see there are several issues you are facing at this time. We've made a good start. After you've had time to sort them out, you may want us to talk again."

"We've covered a lot of ground today . . ."

"I'm glad we had a chance to sit down and talk. You've mentioned a lot of feelings. We've talked about a number of concerns you're having. We've made a start, and I look forward to working on these things with you."

At the end of any of the above, or similar, closing statements, we might ask the client if she would like to go to the appointment desk and set up an appointment to come in again. Or, if on the phone, we can explain to the client that she probably will get another peer counselor the next time she phones, but that is all right—she can simply tell the other counselor what is going on with her at that time.

The "Bomb" at the End of the Session

Occasionally, when the peer counselor is attempting to end the session, the client will suddenly come up with a very serious concern heretofore not mentioned—a "bomb." The concern may be actual, or she may have constructed it for the purpose of maneuvering the peer counselor into extending the session. In either case, we need to proceed with ending the session without ignoring the client's new concern and without apologizing. Generally, no new material should be discussed when it is time to end. We have the right and the responsibility to limit the session to a reasonable time and need to be assertive enough not to be drawn back into the conversation.

Here is an example of a client's bomb at the end of a face-to-face session, and the peer counselor's response:

PEER C: I can see there are several issues you're facing right now. We've made a good start. After you've had time to sort things out a bit, you may want us to talk again.

LIZ: Oh! And I haven't had a chance to tell you. My boss says he's going to fire me if I don't have sex with him.

PEER C: You have just raised an important issue and one we do not have time to do justice to today. Let's hold that off until our next meeting when we can give it our full attention.

Here is an example of a client's bomb at the end of a telephone session, and the peer counselor's response:

PEER C: How about our calling it quits for now? We've covered a lot of ground and had a good conversation.

CLAIRE: I need to talk longer. My mother died last week.

PEER C: I can understand how important that is to you and your need to talk about it, but we have been talking a long time and I need to open the line to other callers. How about your calling back later when I, or another peer counselor, can talk with you when we don't feel rushed?

When the client drops a bomb, we must of course use some discretion. If we judge that the bomb is an authentic emergency (for example, if the client is suicidal or is being physically abused), addressing it cannot be put off. If we have other compelling commitments, the client can be turned over to another volunteer. However, continuity is needed in emergency situations, and we should spend the time, if possible, in providing needed assistance or making appropriate referrals.

If, in our judgment, the request for an extension of time, though not an actual emergency, is a genuine concern that is causing the client great emotional pain, an appointment can be made for the next day. Or, if counseling by telephone, the client can be invited to phone back in a few hours. But remember, the client has been with us long enough for a lengthy conversation and is just now revealing this important issue.

Feeling confident of rights and realizing responsibilities helps us to be assertive without being defensive in these situations. When we are confident that we are being fair, the client usually will accept, without feeling rejected, our insistence that the session end after a reasonable time.

An Ungraceful Ending

But what if the client disregards our efforts to close the session and continues to talk about her difficulties? Such a client seems not to hear our ending statements and just goes on talking, and talking, and talking. Clients who seek peer counseling or use crisis lines often are not as sophisticated as those who pursue professional therapy, and these clients often use every means at their disposal to prolong the session. When this occurs we may as well forget executing a graceful ending and settle for an *un*graceful one. In fact, we may recognize this type of client before time for the session to end and may not even attempt to use a closing statement such as those listed above. Certainly we will not say, "Before we close for today, is there anything else of immediate concern you would like to say?" More sensible closing statements for this type of client are:

"Our time is up."

"We really must go now."

"I have another appointment right now."

"Let's go to the desk and I will find that referral I promised you."

If none of these work, it is perfectly all right, and in fact necessary, to stand up and begin walking out the door as the client continues talking. She will follow.

In telephone counseling, when the client simply will not let go, we can say something to the effect that, "I must open the line to other callers. You may call back later. I'm going to have to hang up now, goodbye," and then hang up.

Summing Up

The above suggestions for ending a session may seem extreme and uncaring. I admit they may be extreme, but I do not think they are uncaring. Neither the client nor the peer counselor profits from prolonging the session indefinitely.

Once the initially allocated amount of time has been used, or when the session clearly is no longer productive, a tactful, deliberate, but definite ending is appropriate. A sense of when the session needs to end, a conviction that ending it on time is right and fair to both client and peer counselor, confidence in knowing a tactful way to end the session, and willingness to end it in an awkward manner, if necessary, provide a firm base for the peer counselor's peace and satisfaction during the session. This in turn contributes to the client's trust and confidence throughout and after the session.

A Look at the Results

When you or I, the peer counselor, work very hard to assist the client and she does not use our assistance, we may feel disappointed or even angry. After all, we have given of ourselves, and she has not accepted our gift. When I have these feelings, I find the following story helpful.

> Some time ago I had almost reached my home after the day's work when a stranger accosted me. He asked me if I knew the whereabouts of a certain street he was looking for. I pointed it out to him, "Straight down and to your left." Assured that I had been understood, I walked on. As I did, I noticed that the stranger was walking in the opposite direction of that I had indicated. "Sir," I said, "you are going in the wrong direction." "I know," he replied, "I am not quite ready yet." [Benjamin 1981, p. 1]

7

Roadblocks to Effective Peer Counseling

Sometimes our natural tendency to avoid difficulties actually creates difficulties. In peer counseling our attempts to evade or bypass problems may in fact hinder the client from working on his problem. Trainees tend to run into the same "pitfalls" or "roadblocks" to effective peer counseling. These roadblocks affect the peer counseling session negatively in that they operate to:

- Minimize or deny the reality of the client's concern.
- Lower the client's self-esteem.
- Invalidate the client's feelings.
- Generate an unwarranted dependence on the peer counselor's ability to resolve the client's dilemma.
- Shame and persuade the client by creating an emotional environment in which he would be most uncomfortable if he did not cooperate.

Before roadblocks can be dismantled, they must be recognized. Listed below are the more common ones.

Advising

The greatest of all roadblocks to effective peer counseling is giving the client advice. Reasons for not giving advice are delineated in detail in Chapter 4 and thus will be noted only briefly here.

Following is an example of how a peer counselor should *not* respond.

MIKE: My wife runs around some with a woman who I don't know very well. I do know the woman's husband, though. He shot a woman and spent time in prison. He's out now, but I hear he's getting in trouble again. I think my wife should stop having anything to do with the woman.

PEER C: If I were you, I'd tell her exactly how I feel.

Agreeing

Peer counselor responses that indicate agreement with the client—for example, "Yes!" "I agree!" "Sure!" "Of course!" or "Naturally!"—may seem like nice, friendly, innocent remarks. We commonly use such responses in our social or business world. But when we agree with the client, we enter into the client's concerns, taking the focus away from him and putting it on ourselves. We are no longer a sounding board exclusively for the client. Our approval and disapproval may become an issue. Wanting our approval, the client may say only what he thinks will gain it. Our indications of agreement tend to derail our efforts to reflect back to him what he is saying and feeling. Consider the following dialogue.

MIKE: I'm not going to let being unemployed get me down. I believe that if I just don't give up, if I keep trying, there is a job out there somewhere for me.

PEER C: I agree.

MIKE: After all, I'm talented and have good skills, and someone out there will appreciate what I have to offer.

PEER C: Of course!

MIKE: So if they don't offer me more money than I was getting on the last job, I'll tell them what they can do with it.

Even when we use the response "yes" to mean "I am listening, go on talking," the client may take it as agreement with what he is saying. When we wish to convey that we heard what the client said and that it is all right for him to continue, the sound "mm-hm" is more appropriate.

Analyzing

A client's present difficulties most likely have some connection with his childhood, and some peer counselors seem to have the knack for seeing the connections between the past and the present. However, to encourage the uprooting of defenses a client has in place would not be helpful to him—and might be harmful. Sometimes a client does get in touch with his own defenses in a peer counseling session, but when this happens it is of his own doing and he generally knows intuitively what he can handle emotionally. We should not, and are not expected to, attempt in-depth analysis. Here is an example of what a peer counselor should not say.

RAY: She said she really liked me and she calls me almost every day. She seems really nice, but I know it is just a matter of time until I learn what the catch is. She may think I am rich. There's always a catch, you know.

PEER C: Sounds like you have really been hurt in the past and that may be causing you to be suspicious of her compliments.

A better response from the peer counselor would be, "You believe there is always a catch."

Digging up and exploring old data is tedious, time consuming, and sometimes scary. It should not be encouraged in peer counseling. In-depth counseling requires the skills of a professional therapist. Owing to the limited time and lack of continuity in the peer counseling setting, even mental health professionals who work as volunteers in a peer counseling capacity would not attempt in-depth analysis.

Anticipating

If the client's story sounds classic, it may be because we are assuming we know the end of his story. If the story seems to drag, we may become impatient and turn our thoughts to what we imagine the client will say next. Here is an example.

PHIL: My wife has always had a good job. She has a college education, and I quit school in the eleventh grade. I drive a taxi. I'm dependable, and they seem to like me where I work. I've been there a long time and I know my way around and I do a good job. My wife has never seemed to be concerned that I don't earn as much as she does.

PEER C: You are good at what you do. Your wife earns more than you do, but she seems quite satisfied with the way things are.

PHIL: But now she's been offered this great job in California. It would mean starting all over and making new friends and everything.

PEER C: She has this job offer, but you are worried about having to find a new job and make new friends.

PHIL: Huh? Whatever made you think that? Actually, I'm very excited about moving to a place I've never been before. She's the one who is worried about making the change.

When we anticipate what the client is going to say next or how his story will end, we are not really listening to him. We lose track of the actual story and are unable to restate precisely what he has said. If we respond to the client by predicting, probably inaccurately, the direction of his thinking, he likely will feel misunderstood.

Assuming or Concluding

One of the things that makes it so difficult to respond appropriately to a client, particularly in reflecting feelings, is that his situation may impact him differently than it would impact us given a similar situation. If we hear the client's story and prematurely conclude the nature of his difficulty, our assumptions may not be true.

For example, we might feel very uncomfortable losing our job, making a presentation to five hundred people, having only enough money to live until next payday, or living a very secluded life. In the same circumstances the client might not feel uncomfortable.

Recently I peer-counseled a mentally disturbed client whose disability was controlled with medication. She told me that her therapist insisted she go to the day center (a social gathering place for the mentally disturbed). Her complaint was that she did not want to go. She went into great detail explaining what was wrong with the place. It was too messy, too noisy, and not well supervised; she had to help clean the place; and her peers there were all "crazy." I responded that it must be lonely for her to be at home by herself all day. She replied, "Oh, no, I like to be alone. I have so much reading to do." And then I realized she had said nothing that would even remotely indicate that she was lonely. I apparently was reflecting how I would feel were I alone all day every day. How easy it is to try to help the old lady cross the street when she does not want to cross the street!

While we must reflect what we perceive the client to be feeling, we must base our perceptions, as much as we can, on what he has said about his difficulty and how he has said it. Believing he feels the way we would feel in his situation may get in the way of productive peer counseling.

Contradicting

Consider the following dialogues:

BOB: If I confront my supervisor, he will fire me.

PEER C: Oh, you can't be sure he would fire you. He might even respect you more.

or

BOB: If she refuses to marry me, I will never be happy.

PEER C: How in the world can you say that? It may seem that way now, but you can't let one person control your life.

Our telling the client we do not believe what he said may make him defensive. It will not convince him his thoughts and feelings are inaccurate. At least we should hope the client does not see us as an authority and hold us responsible for his life.

In the above examples, the client is stating feelings, probably of fear or insecurity. It is better for us to reflect the feelings we perceive him to be feeling than to confirm or deny his statement. The latter may simply close the door to further exploration of his situation.

There is an exception to the rule of not contradicting a client. If it is clear that he is ignorant of a well-known, scientifically proven fact and that his ignorance might affect him adversely, we should of course so inform him. For example, if the teenage client says:

DENNIS: I don't think it's fair that my girlfriend insists on my using a condom the first time we have sex. Everybody knows a girl can't get pregnant the first time she has sex.

PEER C: Dennis, I'm afraid you have been misinformed. A girl can indeed get pregnant the first time she has sex.

Diverting

Regardless of how much we may enjoy our work as a peer counselor, there are days when we would rather not go to work. Perhaps this is one of those days when we feel happy and carefree and had rather sing and dance than be a good listener. Or maybe we talked with this client last week and were particularly moved by his story. We are anxious to see him again and hope that our support will help. But when he comes in, he talks about something entirely different from what he talked about last week. At such times we may attempt to divert the client from what he came in or phoned to talk about.

GEORGE: I am so tired. My wife and I fought all week. You know, I think she may be on drugs. She just goes over and over the same old things, and I was just thinking about how she was when we married, and I believe she may be on drugs.

PEER C: Before we get into that, tell me about that class you wanted to take. Did you sign up?

or

PEER C: I forgot to offer you coffee. Shall I go get us some?

Ignoring

Sometimes the client does not speak clearly or does not put his words together in such a way that we know what he means. Or perhaps our mind was on something else and we weren't listening. When this happens we need to make a quick guess about whether what we missed is critical to the client's story. If it is not, chances are that it is better not to interrupt him for clarification. For example, if he told us the date of his surgery and we don't remember it, it is probably safe to assume this will not impact our understanding of the remainder of what he says. But if what we missed was critical, we must not ignore this gap. Otherwise we are lost and will be unable to respond effectively for the remainder of the session. We must stop him to clarify. For example, we can say:

> "I'm sorry, I don't think I picked up what you said about . . ."
>
> or
>
> "I'm afraid I didn't quite follow what you said just now."
>
> or
>
> "I'm wondering what your comments about . . . mean to you."

The longer we wait, the harder it is to clarify. If we wait a long time, the client will know we have been pretending to hear and his trust will diminish.

Interpreting

We should not interpret why a client says what he says or feels the way he feels. Here is an example of what a well-meaning peer counselor might say.

Tom: I just can't help it. I am so attracted to Kelly. Compared to her, my wife looks like a dog. And she is so much fun to be with. My wife complains all the time and pushes the kids off on me when I get home. I don't know how much longer I can take it. I am seriously thinking of just leaving town with Kelly. I can get a job almost anywhere.

Peer C: Oh, you're just frustrated right now. You're experiencing a mid-life crisis. Many men your age get this urge to begin a new life. You'll get over it.

Interrupting

In Chapter 5 it was stressed that interrupting the client is appropriate when he talks nonstop in the beginning of the session. And in Chapter 6 it was emphasized that, if the client is reluctant to let go at the end of the session, interrupting may be necessary. In the paragraph above on "ignoring," it was suggested that interrupting for clarification might sometimes be necessary. Although these exceptions are valid, the fact is that they *are* "exceptions." In general, interrupting the client not only is impolite, but gets in his way. The client's slowness in talking or in making progress can try our patience, but we can't bring him up to our speed. We can help him most by settling in and really listening without interrupting. With the typical client, there are adequate breaks in his normal flow of words for us to respond without interrupting.

Judging

As we peer-counsel, though our focus is on the client, we do not suddenly cease having thoughts and feelings concerning ourselves. We relate to the client in many ways.

We judge the client's morals. To be nonjudgmental would be to be without values. Most of us have strong opinions about many things—how people should look and act, different aspects of sexuality, religion, abortion, politics, the environment, whether or not to pick up a hitchhiker. Our values may change with time, but for now we feel a certain way. When our client speaks his views concerning moral issues, if his views are different from ours, we think of course that he is wrong. One's values do not suddenly disappear in a peer counseling session. Judging whether his morals are right or wrong is natural and need not interfere with our counseling. The issue here is whether we judge that he could and should think differently. We can believe him to be wrong and at the same time realize that he is sincere and that we cannot know how he came to think the way he does. If we were in his shoes, we might feel as he does. We can realize that he does not have to have our values for us to be supportive of him and that our "helping" does not involve trying to change his values. If we judge the client's morality but feel that we should not judge, our mixed emotions will undoubtedly distract us. And oddly enough, the more indecisive we are about what we believe, the more likely our tentative beliefs are to interfere with our peer counseling. Flimsy beliefs are easily threatened. Being indecisive is different from being flexible. It is being unwilling to risk forming firm beliefs based on what we know right now. We can have very firm beliefs and still be flexible—have a mind open to changing our beliefs should we acquire new data. If our beliefs are firm and we stay aware of them so they cannot slip up on us from behind, and if we feel friendly toward our client's beliefs, being judgmental will not interfere with our peer counseling.

Moralizing

Consider the following client's statement and peer counselor responses:

RANDY: My supervisor was pretty impressed with the report I handed in. It actually was a report my co-worker had done, but my supervisor didn't know the difference.

PEER C: You must know that was unfair.

Peer counselors sometimes feel it their duty to point out immoral acts to the client. Actually, reprimanding the client is not constructive and will just make him defensive.

Consider the following response:

PEER C: You gave your co-worker's report to your supervisor and let her believe it was your own.

This response is factual, but it sounds chastising. A better response would be: "You handed in your co-worker's report as your own. Your supervisor was impressed and did not know the difference."

The effective peer counselor avoids standing moral guard over what the client says. Simply responding to content and reflecting feelings are far more likely to leave the client free to examine his own morals. If we encounter a client who has no sense of what society considers right and wrong, we can be confident that peer counseling will neither socialize him nor benefit him in any other way. The best thing we can do with such a client may be to terminate the conversation and attempt to refer him to a professional therapist.

Overrelating

Another way the peer counselor relates to the client is by empathizing with him. As the client talks and we begin to understand what is going on with him, we to some extent identify with what he says. Identifying with him—being able to partially understand his feelings—is what makes us caring people. Our caring is a positive influence on the session if we retain a strong sense of self. If we care so much that the boundary between us blurs and we can scarcely tell where we end and he begins, if we care more than he does, our caring may be a negative influence on the session. Rather than respecting him as a separate individual, we may begin to feel responsible for him.

Sometimes a peer counselor, because of an unhealed emotional parallel in his or her own life, relates so closely with the client that he or she cannot be objective. It is all right to explain the situation to the client and get another volunteer to work with him.

We may relate to the client by feeling pity, which can have a negative influence on the session. These feelings on our part indicate that we do not respect the client's potential for handling his own difficulty.

Another way the peer counselor may relate to the client is by being angry with him. If we sense that we are becoming angry, it may be that we are allowing the client to take advantage of us. We may not have been assertive enough in keeping the client focused. Or it could be that we need to terminate the session but are not doing so. Or we might become angry when a female client tells us her husband beats her but that she still loves him and plans to stay with him. In this case we may be angry *for* her, or we may be angry at the unfairness of the situation. Whatever the reason, being aware of our anger leaves us in control of it.

The peer counselor may relate to the client by wanting his approval. It could be that the volunteer is the type of person who needs everyone's approval. Here again, if we are aware of our needs we will be in charge of them and can choose our actions rather than react to them.

Or it could be the client reminds the peer counselor of someone else he or she knows or has known. The counselor may transfer what were his or her feelings toward that person to the client. The client can experience the same thing. He may like or dislike us because we remind him of someone else he knows, or someone in his past. Knowing that transference can happen may help us to identify, and thus handle, feelings that might otherwise not have been recognized.

We do not need to deny our feelings during the counseling session. We do not even need to be free from irrational feelings. Who is? The key to constructive handling of the different ways we relate to the client is simply to stay aware of our feelings. If we keep an eye on our feelings as we would on dynamic, energetic children in our care, we will be in charge of our emotions and they will not impede our peer counseling.

Praising

Unlike most of the roadblocks listed in this chapter, praising, while it *can* be a roadblock, is not necessarily so. Actually, whether or not to praise a client is probably the most controversial issue in the training of peer counselors. Proponents say clients have low self-esteem and need praise. Those opposed point out that peer counselors would never condemn the client, and that praising is just as intrusive in terms of entering our opinions.

In some counseling agencies the term *stroke* is used to denote praise, and stroking is encouraged. As a peer counselor trainee, my first confused response to this term was that the trainers were referring to a seizure. I soon realized that they were talking about an intimacy of caressing or petting, as in cuddling a kitten. This seemed to me, when applied to humans, to be at best belittling, and at worst degrading. Perhaps those trainers who teach stroking avoid calling the act "praising" because this would clearly signify that the peer counselor is entering his or her opinion into the session. I believe it is imperative, in order to encourage the use of appropriate caution, that we call it like it is.

Praise is different from affirmation. Affirmation is the acceptance of and respect for the client as a person of intrinsic, inherent worth and is not dependent upon his virtues or accomplishments. Affirmation occurs when the peer counselor listens attentively to the client, attempts to understand his story from his frame of reference, and responds to him in a way that demonstrates that he was heard and accepted.

Praise is a compliment based on our personal opinion, which is formed by our value system. It is a judgment reflecting our perception and comes from our frame of reference. When we praise a client we are indeed entering ourselves, our opinions, our values into the session. We are rewarding the client for following our values. When we bestow praise we take the risk that the client will screen his story and tell us only what he thinks will reinforce our approval of him.

In spite of all those good reasons for not praising a client, I tend to believe we should. My justification (or rationalization) is that most clients are people who get so little praise in their day-to-day life, so seldom have their virtues noticed by others, and so often have their shortcomings, mistakes, and liabilities brought to their attention. They are yelled at, put down, stomped on, or—worse—ignored. I believe a bit of praise from us simply helps to balance the scales.

But when we choose to praise the client, we should do so with painstaking scrupulousness. There are four considerations to keep in mind.

1. The praise must be genuine. We must not give praise out of a wish or a need to make the client feel better at any cost. We must believe what we are saying and he must find it believable.
2. We must have information that will support our opinion. It must be something we know to be true. Since we cannot know if what the client says is true, this pretty much limits our praise to something we see for ourselves in the session—for example, the client's determination, hard work, perseverance, skill at verbalizing, or some other attribute that we are in a position to see.

I once heard a peer counselor say on the telephone, "You are a very good mother." No doubt the motive was compassion and caring, but he did not have sufficient information to know whether this client was a good mother. The client may even have thought she was not a good mother, in which case the compliment would have made her feel inadequate or guilty. And most certainly the praise would have prevented her from talking about what a poor mother she felt she was.

3. The information with which we back our compliment must pertain to the work of the counseling session. It is not appropriate, for example, to comment on the client's physical appearance (unless that is what the counseling session is about).

Here is an example of what can happen if we give a compliment that is not related to the business at hand.

PEER C: That is a lovely sweater you have on, Jane.

JANE: Thank you. I got it on sale at Macy's. They have such a terrific sale going on you just can't miss it. There also were some beautiful skirts and blouses and they still had a good selection of colors and sizes. What size do you wear?

Jane comes in again the following week and begins the session by saying:

JANE: You know that sweater I wore last week? Well, I went back and got another in a different color. It washes well and the price was incredible. Have you had a chance to go there this week? I saw this little blouse that I bet you would just love. It is just your color and size. What time do you get off work here? I could go with you and show it to you.

Even though we are *peer* counselors, our work is more efficient if we act professionally. Our volunteer hours are for helping people who are experiencing difficulties in their lives. Socializing gets in the way.

4. The client must be in a position to believe what we say. If the client is depressed or has an overall negative attitude, our complimenting him, though sincere, will probably not

be perceived as authentic but rather as an attempt to make him feel better.

Adhering to these guidelines obviously limits the praise we can give a client, but I suspect a bit of genuine praise, well received, is a nugget of gold that nourishes the client's hungry heart.

Probing

In an effort to encourage a client to "open up," some peer counselors use a response such as one of the following.

"Tell me more."
"Tell me what happened then."
"Tell me again exactly what happened when you . . ."
"I would like to know more about . . ."

Whose needs are we satisfying here? When we probe the client thus, we are inserting ourselves into the session by suggesting the direction of the conversation. By such responses we are taking the lead, and probably causing the client to begin looking to us for what should happen next.

I remember observing a trainee in a role play saying to his pretend client, "Tell me more." The role-play client stopped dead in his tracks, his spontaneity squelched. There was silence as he tried to think of what more he could say about what he just said. After the role play ended, during "feedback" time, the role-play client said he wasn't sure what happened but that he never quite got around to what he really wanted to talk about. Genuine opening up comes only in the client's own time, at his own speed, and in response to his feeling safe and accepted. These things are facilitated by the peer counselor's simply listening and responding.

Questioning

A vital ingredient of the helping process is for the client to feel free to talk about and explore his concerns any way he wishes. When we ask a question, we risk interrupting his train of thought and possibly leading him away from what he came in, or phoned, to talk about. Our questioning may result in leaving his real issues untouched. When we ask a question, we are taking the lead in the conversation, causing it to focus on what *we* think is important rather than what *he* thinks is important. The typical client, erroneously thinking the peer counselor knows better than he what issues should be addressed, will follow our lead, answer our questions as best he can, and, in return for his correct answer, expect us to give him solutions to his problems. After all, this is how he responds to and get answers from his physician or attorney.

Asking the client questions, especially in the beginning of the session, can set a precedent: we ask the questions, he gives the answers. This can derail the helping process and make it difficult to get back on track.

Asking a question can be an indirect way of advising the client. For example, we might say, "Before you phone the police about your neighbor beating his wife, are you going to go over and talk to him about it?" Although this might be in the form of a question, it may be perceived by the client as the peer counselor's advising him to talk with his neighbor before taking more drastic action.

When we attempt to help the client get in touch with his feelings, it may seem that the most straightforward way is simply to ask, "How do you feel about that?" It is certainly straightforward enough, but may not be helpful. The client may not be ready to get in touch with his feelings. He may not know how he feels and, feeling he should know, feel inadequate. As detailed in Chapter 3, a better way to help him get in touch with his feelings is to reflect back to him what we perceive him to be feeling. This invites, but does not demand, his getting in touch with his feelings.

And just when we think we have mastered the art of not asking questions, we find we may ask them inadvertently by ending a statement response with a vocal inflection, thus turning a response statement into a question. For example:

AMOS: I just don't know what job I should take.

PEER C: You are having trouble deciding between them?

or

You are frustrated?

Such responses can lead the client to attempt to answer our unintended questions rather than get on with his story.

The exception to the rule that we should not ask a client questions appears in Chapter 4. When using this decision-making process, questions are appropriate. In that situation, the questions evolve from the client's frame of reference and are used—with the client's permission—to lead him through the steps of the process. Asking questions is also warranted in emergency situations, as detailed in Chapter 10.

Why is it so difficult for new peer counselors to refrain from asking questions? We depend on questions to foster social conversation: "What do you do?" (meaning how do you make a living). "Where do you live? "Who are your significant others?" Without such questions, many people would be at a loss for words. In peer counseling we may ask questions because we are accustomed to doing so, or we may do so because asking questions is simply easier than listening well and restating or reflecting.

Before we ask the client a question, a good rule is to ask ourselves why we need to know and what we are going to do with the information once we get it. We do not need to know about the client; he needs to know about himself.

Reasoning

If the client makes what appears to be unreasonable or illogical statements, we might be tempted to insert reason or logic into the session. However, attempting to reason with the client may create an atmosphere in which he is not only disaffirmed but also made to feel uncomfortable if he does not agree with our reasoning.

JEFF: I'm so confused! First she says one thing, and then she turns right around and does the opposite. I'm so angry! She won't get away with this. Oh! I feel like I'm going crazy!

PEER C: The best thing you can do in a situation like this is to stay calm. Don't overreact. When you get so upset like this, you can't accomplish anything.

When the client invites us to listen, and we tell him why he should not feel the way he does, we trample his feelings. Attempting to insert logic does not help him come to terms with his feelings; in fact, it may do the opposite by introducing new feelings of inadequacy or guilt.

Suppose the conversation had gone this way:

JEFF: I'm so confused! First she says one thing, and then she turns right around and does the opposite. I'm so angry! She won't get away with this. Oh! I feel like I'm going crazy!

PEER C: I can see why you'd feel like you're going crazy. It's a tough situation. You have a right to feel the way you feel.

Again, the peer counselor is attempting to apply logic to the client's feelings. He or she is giving a personal opinion about the client's feelings instead of reflecting them. A better response is: "You're feeling frustrated and angry." Such a response is more likely to cause the client to accept his feelings and get beyond them.

Consider still another dialogue demonstrating reasoning with the client.

JOE: I have thought about it a lot, and I don't think I will have the operation after all.

PEER C: Your physician says that you have to have it. You know, you really don't have a choice. You won't get better without it.

In this dialogue the peer counselor is pushing his values on the client. The client doesn't really have to have the surgery. He does have a choice. Telling the client he must have the surgery will not change these facts. But in this example even greater harm may result from the client's likely perception that his true feelings are being ignored. What he may have been trying to say is, "I really dread having that surgery." This is how the dialogue might have gone.

JOE: I've thought about it a lot, and I don't think I will have the operation after all.

PEER C: You're worried about the prospect of having the operation.

Reassuring

Consider the following peer counseling dialogue:

ANDY: I was thinking of applying for a job, but I know nobody would hire me.

PEER C: Of course they would!

or

ANDY: I believe if I applied for that job, I would get it.

PEER C: Go for it!

or

ANDY: I just know my girlfriend doesn't love me.

PEER C: Of course she does!

or

ANDY: I think I'll just give up. I've tried five times and couldn't do it.

PEER C: Oh, you'll be able to do it eventually! Just look at how well you do everything else.

or

ANDY: I have to go to the hospital tomorrow for some test. I sure dread hearing the results.

PEER C: It probably won't be as bad as you think.

or

ANDY: Seems like everything is going wrong. I just don't know what I'm going to do.

PEER C: Don't worry. Everything's going to be all right.

The above peer counselor's promises may be well intentioned, but they are unsubstantiated. They tell the client he is wrong, that he does not know his own mind. If he believes the counselor, he may feel guilty for feeling the way he does, which may discourage him from looking squarely at what is causing his distress.

If we are tempted to reassure the client by giving him a little pep talk, we might ask ourselves why we want to do this. Could it be that we wish to avoid hurting with the client?

Rescuing

Consider the following dialogue:

GARY: I've been thinking lately about where my life is going. It seems to be going nowhere. I just go to this dead-end job every day, go home at the end of the day, watch TV, and go to bed. Every Friday I bring my paycheck home to my wife and children. It seems I don't really *know* my children. I guess I should spend more time with them.

PEER C: But when you come home at the end of the day, I know you must be very tired.

This peer counselor probably was trying to make Gary feel better, but she sacrificed the session by discrediting what he said. She is attempting to rescue Gary, to excuse him from the need to explore his concerns. In effect, she is insinuating that he may be incapable of dealing with his concerns. Melody Beattie, in her book *Codependent No More*, says: "Caretaking looks like a much friendlier act then it is. It requires incompetency on the part of the person being taken care of. We rescue 'victims'—people who we believe are not capable of being responsible for themselves" (1987, p. 79).

Taking Sides

Many clients blame their predicament on someone else. They believe so strongly in their own innocence that they make a very convincing case. A peer counselor who is inclined toward analyzing may find himself or herself trying to decide who is to blame and communicate this to the client.

LARRY: My employer gives me these projects to do but he doesn't make clear what he really wants. Every time, he waits until I'm finished and then tells me what's wrong with what I've done. It's really frustrating.

PEER C: I can see how that would really be frustrating—it's so unfair.

Here is another version of the same scenario.

JEFF: I just finished college and was fortunate enough to get a good job already. I assumed I would move back in with my parents, but they are asking me to pay rent! Can you imagine? Pay rent in my own home? How am I going to pay rent and have enough for all my other expenditures? I just bought a new sports car and I have to make payments, you know.

PEER C: But you are a working adult now. You would have to pay rent to live anywhere else.

Taking sides, either with the client or with those about whom he speaks, has no place in peer counseling. We need to stay with the client's thoughts and feelings.

Using Personal Examples

Sometimes a client will relate an experience that seems so much like one of ours that we are tempted to offer ours as an example.

MARIE: I had my heart set on having a baby, one of my very own. When I moved in with Mark six months ago I assumed he would want a baby too, but he says he doesn't. And he's so good with my nieces and nephews. I mean, who would have thought? What am I going to do?

PEER C: My husband was exactly the same way. He didn't want me to have one, but after it came, he was so happy. And he's very good with it.

MARIE: How many children do you have?

PEER C: Two.

MARIE: How nice. How old are they?

Notice that, when the peer counselor took the lead by turning the focus on herself, the client followed suit. It will now be difficult to focus the session back on the client.

Their dialogue also could have gone like this:

MARIE: I had my heart set on having a baby, one of my very own. When I moved in with Mark six months ago I assumed he would want a baby too, but he says he doesn't. And he's so good with my nieces and nephews. I mean, who would have thought? What am I going to do?

PEER C: My husband was exactly the same way. At first he didn't want me to have one, but after it came, he was so happy. And he's so good with it.

MARIE: You know, my aunt told me the same thing. She said my boyfriend couldn't help but love it when it came. I think I'll take your advice and go ahead and get pregnant. Mark has been threatening to leave me, but I bet he wouldn't if we had a baby.

It would be interesting to see how the peer counselor in the latter dialogue handles the remaining time with her client.

Admittedly, other scenarios might not have such a potentially damaging effect on the client's life. However, the fact that we are not professional therapists seems not to deter clients from seeing us as authorities. With this standing goes the responsibility for avoiding personal examples.

Words to Avoid

Following are some terms to shun when responding to clients.

1. *I understand.* We don't really. No one can fully understand another person. Although our wish is to convey that we understand (somewhat), respect what he is saying, and empathize, a better way to convey this message is to restate what he is saying or reflect what he is feeling.
2. *Why? Why did you do that? Why did you say that? Why do you feel that way?* These interjections come through to many as accusations. Peer counselors never really need to know why.
3. *Problem.* Generally, problems are to be solved. The peer counselor does not focus on solving problems. Better words to use are *difficulty, transition, dilemma, predicament, quandary, issue, concern, situation, circumstance,* or *crisis.* If the client uses the word "problem," of course, we may also use it.
4. *Normal.* "Normal" is closely associated with "abnormal." A better word is "natural." It is not helpful to the client for us to suggest his behavior, or situation, is either "normal" or "abnormal."

Summing Up

Most of the above roadblocks have one thing in common: the emphasis shifts—the peer counselor moves from the frame of reference of the client to his or her own. The client becomes the follower. Although falling into the trap of using these roadblocks takes away from the effectiveness of the counseling session, it is understandable. The roadblocks reflect ordinary responses that generally serve us well in family, social, or business communications. However, by slipping into these responses, the peer counselor is in effect saying to the client, "Since you are incompetent, I must take a leading role in addressing your difficulty." The client, though possibly unable to verbalize his feelings, senses that he is being put off, put down, or told what to do.

If we hear ourselves doing most of the talking, we well may have collided with a roadblock. We may need to back up and proceed with caring and caution!

8

Other Things You Need to Know

While the preceding chapter is mostly about what *not* to do as a peer counselor, this chapter emphasizes what *to* do. The intent here is to provide information to those who already have the basic skills and are ready to learn how to respond constructively to a variety of counseling situations not covered, or only lightly covered, in earlier chapters. This chapter is about how to be a more professional nonprofessional.

Assessing Needs

As peer counselors, we should always begin our initial contact with the client by listening and responding to the content of what she says. Listening serves two purposes. First, it provides information on which to base our responses to content and, second, it helps us pick up on needs the client may have other than or in addition to peer counseling. Some of these needs might be so great that they require priority attention, for example, the need for medical treatment, food, shelter, transportation, safety from an abusing spouse, child care, and suicide intervention.

If we suspect that the client's major need is for other than peer counseling, we should discontinue being nondirective, at least for the moment, and take the lead in the conversation, becoming directive, asking questions, and gathering information until the client's priority need has been determined. In assessing needs, it may be helpful to remember that as peer counselors we have only three avenues via which to assist the client in meeting her needs. These are:

1. Peer counseling
2. Referrals to other community agencies or professionals
3. Responses to emergencies or other "special cases" needs

Assessing needs, then, is primarily a matter of determining which avenue is appropriate for this particular client at this particular time. If we determine that the client's need cannot be addressed by one or more of these avenues, our only recourse is to inform the client that our agency is not set up to assist with her particular need.

If the client's need really is for peer counseling, we are off to a good start. Since we started the conversation by peer counseling, we can simply continue in this same mode. If the client needs a referral to another community agency or a professional, we can switch into a more directive mode and provide the appropriate referral. If the client is in an emergency situation or in one of the other "special cases" categories, we will switch into a more directive mode of taking charge, asking questions, giving instructions, or in some cases (such as with the terminally ill) simply offer emotional support. (Referring is discussed further in the next subsection; handling emergencies and other special cases is covered in Chapter 10.)

The following example demonstrates the peer counselor's assessing needs and acting upon a need for a referral.

PEER C: Hello. This is the crisis line.

MARTHA: Hello. I just need to talk to someone.

PEER C: I'll be glad to talk with you.

MARTHA: Well, I don't know what I am going to do. Things are really bad. You can hear my baby crying. She cries a lot. This is not a happy home. My husband lost his job. He is out looking but he can't find work. (*Client cries.*)

PEER C: It's okay to cry. I'll just wait.

MARTHA: I wish I could look for a job too, but I don't have anybody to keep the baby. I don't have any relatives here, and we can't afford a sitter. We can't pay the rent and I don't know what we are going to do about supper tonight.

PEER C: You're wishing you had someone to look after the baby so you could look for a job. You mentioned you don't know what you're going to do about supper tonight. I am wondering just what you meant by that.

MARTHA: There is no food in the house. I don't even have milk for the baby. Oh, what am I going to do?

PEER C: Sounds like you are really in a tight spot right now. Before we talk more, let me tell you of some places you might get food. Do you have a pencil and paper?

The peer counselor then looks on the referral file and gives the client names of agencies that provide emergency food and talks with her about transportation to get the food. She is invited to phone back, after her immediate needs are met, just to talk or to obtain other possible resources that might assist in paying the rent or in helping her husband find employment.

Notice that nondirective peer counseling ceased immediately upon learning of the need for referrals. As noted in Chapter 1, basic physical needs come first. However, it is important to let the client know there is a place where she can talk and deal with her emotional difficulties once her physical needs are met.

More often it happens the other way 'round—a client will ask for a referral because she is reluctant to admit she is emotionally troubled and needs to talk with someone about feelings.

PEER C: Crisis line.

LOIS: Could you give me a referral to a support group?

PEER C: Yes, we have some support groups in our file. Could you tell me a little about what type of support group you are interested in.

LOIS: Well, maybe, like when people are getting a divorce.

PEER C: I think we do have some support groups for people who are separated or divorced. Are *you* recently divorced or thinking of getting a divorce?

LOIS: Well, I just learned something my husband has been doing, and I just can't live with him. (*She begins crying.*)

PEER C: Take your time. (*Pause, then softly speaks*) You're saying you have just learned something your husband has been doing that causes you to feel like you can't continue living with him.

LOIS: He is doing the worst thing you can imagine. I caught him in bed with my sister.

Obviously this client did not want a referral to a support group—at least not right now. She needed to talk. Any time a client asks for a referral, it is appropriate for the peer counselor to ask her more about her request. This information is needed not only for selecting an appropriate referral but also to help determine whether a referral is really appropriate. But no matter what our suspicions, we need to begin the session wearing our peer nondirective counseling hat. Consider still another scenario.

PEER C: Hello. This is the women's center.

NANCY: Hello. I just need to talk to somebody.

PEER C: I will be glad to talk with you.

NANCY: Well, it's like this. My husband just left, so I can talk now. We've been having lots of trouble lately. Like, I mean he's got a bad temper and he gets real mad.

PEER C: Your husband gets real angry with you.

NANCY: Yeah. And I don't think I did anything wrong. (*Begins crying*)

PEER C: It's okay to take your time. I can tell you are very upset right now. (*Silence of about ten seconds*) You were saying your husband gets angry with you when you think you did nothing wrong.

NANCY: (*Screaming*) Yeah! And it hurts! It hurts! I'm bleeding. I think he broke my nose. What am I going to do? I'm bleeding all over. [How to proceed further with emergency cases is addressed in Chapter 10.]

When a client first begins talking, we should never assume that she has no need other than to talk.

Referring

The client often lacks knowledge of community resources and has little understanding of which sources might be appropriate to meet her immediate needs. Peer counselors can be very helpful in this respect. We may provide a referral at her request or realize her need for a referral as we talk with her. It is appropriate to ask the client if she wishes a referral rather than to assume she does. Our job is to offer, not to push.

Most volunteer agencies that utilize peer counselors have good referral files that contain information about available community agencies and professionals. Although peer counselors are not expected to remember all possible referral sources, we are expected to be proficient in accessing the sources in the file. And if we are really conscientious, we will make ourselves reasonably familiar with sources most likely to be needed in emergency situations (for example, shelters for youth; shelters for abused women; hospitals, particularly the ones who take indigent patients; agencies or churches that offer emergency food; agencies that treat persons who are on drugs; the magistrate's office; the poison control center; "safe" places for children; and the county mental health department). Emergency numbers are listed in the front of some telephone directories. Offices of federal, state, county, and city governments are also listed there. Public libraries often have comprehensive referral files and a staff person skilled at providing referral information.

If the client has multiple needs, we should first determine and focus on her priority need. As a rule, a single referral is all she can process at one time. We can mention that other resources are available if the initial referral does not work out and remind her that she can phone for additional information at any time.

Use of a headphone is convenient when looking up referrals. It enables us to maintain contact with the client and keep her posted as we search. In its absence, some ingenious peer counselors are able to balance the phone on their shoulder and talk to the client while looking for the resource. But there is nothing wrong with putting the client on hold while we search. Sometimes a new peer counselor gets flustered when he or she cannot find a resource right away. There is no need to rush. After all, we are doing the client a service. If she is serious about wanting the referral, she will wait. Also, it is not imperative that we have an appropriate referral. Services simply do not exist to cover every possible need.

The client sometimes asks the peer counselor to phone a community agency or professional for her. We should not do this.

If the client wants the service badly enough, she will phone directly. If she doesn't really want it, she might not take advantage of the available assistance even if we were to make all the necessary arrangements for her. Doing the client's work for her not only encourages her to be dependent, but also could have a negative impact on the reputation of the agency that employs us. For example, if we make an appointment for her, she may not keep it. This may reflect negatively on us. If *she* makes the appointment, she will feel more ownership of the situation and will be held accountable if she does not follow through. As a general rule, we should never do anything for the client that she can do for herself. However, particular clients and particular situations call for an extraordinary amount of our assistance. The client may be suicidal, physically abused, or need emergency shelter, and as a result of her need be so severely distressed that she is unable to communicate or would have difficulty in following through.

Although the referral file of the counselor's agency will probably list names and information about other community agencies, it is unlikely to list names of private therapists, physicians, or attorneys. Nonetheless, many private professionals have grouped together and set up their own referral organizations (e.g., attorney referral service, medical society, mental health association). Contact information for such organizations can usually be found just before listings for that particular group of professionals in the yellow pages of the telephone directory. These referral services are generally better equipped than we are to refer our client to a private professional. They know who is taking new patients or clients and are familiar with the various specialties in their field. Also, the persons answering their phones are trained to ask the right questions to determine which professional would be best for a particular client. For these reasons it is best for the peer counselor to provide the client who needs a referral to a private professional with contact information for the appropriate referral agency.

In referring our client to other referral agencies, we need to be particularly careful that she does not feel pushed out or that we are "passing the buck." Time should be taken to explain why we are referring her to another referral service. Also, this is a good time to describe our own agency's primary services. She should be invited to phone again if she is unable to get a satisfactory referral from the source we give her, and invited to phone back if she just wants to talk to someone about a concern. If the caller insists she wants only the referral, we need to comply with her wishes; however, it is better for us to risk being a bore than to give the client the impression she is being bumped from one agency to another just to get rid of her.

If no appropriate referral agency is available, we can direct our client to the yellow pages of the phone book, giving her the page number on which the particular type of professional she wants is listed. If she insists on our giving her the name of a professional, we should give three. This prevents our agency from appearing to show partiality to one particular professional.

Sometimes the client cannot afford private professional assistance and has needs for which no public help is available or the waiting lists are long. All we can do in these instances is to say we know of no available public assistance. Even then, we can help the client sort out her concerns and help her try to come up with options. Sometimes family or friends might help, but the client may be reluctant to call on them. In these cases our assisting the client in looking at her options may help her see that calling on family or friends is the only viable option.

Helping the Client Focus

Much has been said in previous chapters about the benefits of— the necessity of—the client's leading the conversation. This does not mean, however, that the peer counselor should let the client wander aimlessly throughout the session. While it is up to the client to set the agenda, our job as facilitator is to help her adhere to it. Letting her ramble, or get off on a tangent, is not helpful to her.

Until we listen for a while, we cannot know what her agenda is; we cannot help her focus until we know the focus. So our first job is to listen well, responding to content and reflecting feelings, until we get some sense of the theme of her story.

Sometimes the client may seem to be unfocused or off track when she is not. For example, she may know something is bothering her but be confused as to exactly what it is. She may say she is anxious or bored, or feels as if life is passing her by. We need not—should not—try to analyze the basis for her feelings. For purposes of peer counseling, the difficulty has already surfaced. For the moment, her difficulty is that she feels something is wrong and is unable to determine exactly what it is. So her perplexity is what we address.

Sometimes the client may seem to be unfocused or off track simply because her concerns seem insignificant to the counselor. One of my co-workers at a crisis line, a male approximately 50 years old, listened to a teenage girl tell of her distress at not having a date for the high school prom. In a prior call that day he had spent over an hour on the phone helping a suicidal client find enough hope to hang on for at least a few more days; in another call he had talked with a mother who had just lost a teenager in an automobile accident. It took him a few minutes to "tune in" to what, to this teenager, was a devastating disaster in her life. I was impressed with the way he skillfully shifted gears and related to the teenager's devastation.

Often, however, after we have listened patiently and deliberated thoughtfully, we may come to the conclusion that the client is indeed unfocused or off track. In this case, confronting her is better than allowing her to continue her aimless meandering. Following are seven symptoms that indicate the client is unfocused or off track and examples of possible confrontations.

- *The client goes into trifling detail.* I once talked with a client on the phone who began reading to me an article from a newspaper that vaguely had to do with what she was talking about. I said, "I must stop you now to let you know we do not have enough time to go into that much detail. I am here to help you clarify your thinking and get in touch with your feelings. Earlier you were saying . . ."

- *The client tells another person's story.* For example:

LINDA: My sister had an experience similar to mine except she quit her job. Her co-worker came on to her and when she went to her boss complaining about it, he said the co-worker probably didn't mean anything by it. I think she should have sued. My sister is like that. She never would stand up for herself. She lets her husband run all over her. Just last week he . . ."

PEER C: Let me stop you for a minute. We seem to have drifted away from what you came in [or phoned] to talk about. This is *your* time to talk about *your* issues. Earlier you were saying . . ."

The peer counselor needs to be firm and repeat this or a similar response each time the client begins telling another's story.

- *The client turns the focus onto the peer counselor.* A client sometimes asks the peer counselor personal questions—his or her name and where she or he lives or works. We should not answer personal questions about ourselves. Doing so takes the focus away from the session and provides the client with information she has no right to have. She could use the information to disadvantage by phoning or visiting the peer counselor at home or work. (The peer counselor usually gives his or her first name to face-to-face clients; typically, a name is not given in telephone counseling.) To a client's inappropriate request for personal information, we can simply cite relevant agency policy. On a crisis line, if the client asks for our name so she can talk with us during future calls, we can explain that peer counselors are volunteers who work only a few hours each week and that the crisis line is not set up for a client to get a specific person when she calls.

Sometimes a client compliments the peer counselor on his or her clothes, physical features, or good insight and counseling skills. When this occurs, a simple "Thank you" on our part is sufficient, after which we can return our attention to the session.

Clients often ask the peer counselor questions such as "How would you feel in my situation?" or "What would you do in my situation?" When asked a question, our natural reaction is to begin thinking of an answer. In peer counseling, when we are asked a question, our reaction needs to be, "What is going on with the client to cause her to ask such a question?" What is going on with her may be that she is trying to say one or more of the following:

"How am I going to solve my problem?"
"I am not strong enough to deal with this."
"I wish someone would give me a magic answer."
"I wish someone understood my pain."
"I wonder what others would feel or do in my situation."
"Are my feelings legitimate and my decisions sensible?"

An appropriate response to such questions is to reflect the content or feelings. For example:

"You're wondering what you are going to do."
or
"You wish someone had a magic answer."

Typically, the client does not expect—and probably is not ready for—an answer to such questions and is oblivious to the interchange. Once the peer counselor responds to the content and reflects feelings, the session usually is back on course. However, if the client insists that she meant the question literally, a good response is:

> "It is impossible for me to know how I would feel if I were you, because I am not you. But your feelings are legitimate. It is okay for you to feel the way you do."

The classic response, "What would be right for me probably would not be right for you," leaves the door wide open for the client's likely counter, "Tell me what would be right for you."

If the client is adamant—"I called you for help and you are not giving me answers!"—a good response is:

> "There is no way I can know what is right for you. Only you can decide that. Often just talking about a concern—getting it out in the open where you can look at it—helps to think it through. My job is to listen to you and help you clarify your thoughts."

- *The client talks mostly about her past.* The client sometimes will get off track regarding her present concerns by talking at length about what happened in her past, particularly during her childhood. To talk briefly about her past or her childhood may be a natural part of telling her story. Most clients, in the beginning of the peer counseling session, give a short history of their present concern, which sometimes includes information about their past. The client may, however, attempt in-depth analyzing of her own feelings or may believe she is expected to use this approach to work on her difficulties. It is the peer counselor's obligation to keep the session focused on present concerns. Examples of appropriate responses are:

"What concerns are you having right now that seem connected
to these things that happened in the past?"
or
"How do these things affect your life today?

or
"What triggered these thoughts right now?"
or
"I am wondering what happened today that caused you to
   think of these things."

With a prompt such as one of these, most clients will return
to the here-and-now and begin working on their present concerns and feelings. However, an occasional client will reiterate
old hurts and grievances. She may be invested in blaming her
present troubles on her past. In the peer counseling setting, where
the pain cannot be professionally analyzed and dealt with, this is
not helpful to the client. The peer counselor may need to explain:

> "I am not a professional therapist and therefore not equipped to
> deal with deep-seated issues of your past. Let's see if I can be of
> help concerning what is going on with you now. Earlier, you were
> saying . . ."

If this does not bring the client back to the present, a referral to a
professional therapist is in order.

- *The client contradicts herself.* Sometimes the client will make
  contradictory statements because she changes her mind as
  the session progresses. Often, however, her thinking is so
  unfocused that she is unaware of the conflicts. Ideally, after
  we have listened long enough to have a good grasp of the
  direction the session is taking, we will be in a position to
  judge whether she is in a growth mode and has simply
  changed her mind about some of her concerns or is simply confused or having mixed feelings. If we think the
  former, it might be better to ignore the contradictions. New
  growth is sometimes fragile. However, if she seems to be
  confused, it might help her focus if we call the contradic-

tions to her attention. In responding to the contradictory content, we do not have to limit ourselves to responding to what the client said just a minute ago. We can respond to what she said earlier in the session, or last week, if it is linked with or contradicts what she is saying now. Responding to earlier client statements can be affirming as it demonstrates careful listening and remembering. This method of responding can also help the client see the lack of logic in her statements and help her focus on reality.

Here is an example of a peer counselor's response to a client's contradictory statement:

PEER C: I hear you saying divorcing your husband is inevitable, while in an earlier statement you said you could never leave him. I am wondering if you are having mixed feelings.

- *The client wanders aimlessly.* A client will sometimes bounce from one seemingly unrelated subject to another, presenting such a vague, bewildering, and confusing story that we cannot possibly follow her train of thought. All we can do in such cases is patiently try to follow her, restating the fragments of her story and reflecting the insinuated feelings her tone of voice implies. Then, as we begin to see a trace of why she sought peer counseling, we may realize she is going into so much detail, or is distracted by so many side paths, that she is never going to be able to tell her main story in the fifty minutes or so allotted for the session. In fact, at the rate she is going, it might take hours, or days, or forever. She may be well aware of the general direction of her concerns, but not be able to pinpoint them.

   With this type of client, many interruptions and summary feedbacks are in order. She needs to know she has been listened to, that she has been heard. But we cannot really hear if we cannot comprehend. Again, we do not need to limit ourselves to responding exclusively to what she said a minute ago. In fact, to make sense of her story, we necessarily will sift through the vagueness and details for the kernel of her concern. But we do need to check with her constantly to make sure our summary is accurate. Bringing some organization to her rambling by sifting out the minor ideas and focusing on the major ones may be our best way of helping her. She may be able to take her first constructive step toward addressing her concerns, the step of seeing her concern more clearly.

- *The client is off track for no discernible reason.* If the client is clearly wandering, but the reason for her failure to stay on track is not clear to us, we sometimes can find a focal point by taking the client back to the time she made the appointment or picked up the phone to call.

> "I am wondering what was going on the day you made the appointment to come in [or just before you phoned us] that caused you to seek peer counseling."

Once, after trying unsuccessfully for quite a while to get a handle on why the client phoned, I approached the issue by telling her I was wondering what happened today that prompted her to phone. She answered: "Today is the first anniversary of my mother's death." She then began weeping and talking about how she felt she should be finished grieving but was not.

Another approach to helping the client focus is a direct confrontation:

> "We have been talking for some time now, about many things, and frankly, I don't think I understand what brought you here today [or prompted you to phone]. In order for me to be of assistance to you, I need you to enlighten me a bit."

With all of the above, another tactic that is sometimes helpful to a client who has trouble focusing is to approach her with the decision-making model outlined in Chapter 4. This may not work, but it is worth a try. If the client does not utilize this approach, it may at least bring to her attention that she does not seem to know what she wants.

Seeing that the client stays somewhat on track requires patience and deliberation on the part of the peer counselor. At times it also demands the boldness to risk intervening at what might be an inappropriate time. There is greater risk, however, in our taking an overly passive role. Little that is constructive happens when the client is off track. Once into the session, if it is obvious that the client is not utilizing our efforts to keep her on track, the session should be terminated.

Although assisting the client in focusing and staying on track is important, a word of caution is in order. While we should help her stay focused and on track, we should never attempt to force her to do so. We must be careful not to bulldoze through her confusion by aggressively giving her a crystal clear vision of her concerns. The fog surrounding her difficulty may be her needed defense. She may be emotionally unable to handle a clear vision. So it behooves us not to get caught up in doing such a "great job" of keeping her on track that we destroy her mask. We will not interfere with her safety valve if we stick to the basic peer counseling principles, repeating only what she said, softly and patiently summarizing and reflecting perceived feelings, and waiting to see if she has heard. If it appears that she did not hear us, we need to respond with affirmative, nonthreatening, short continuers and wait awhile to respond to content or feeling. Sometimes such a client benefits from our listening and responding only after the session is over and she has had time to reflect quietly on what has happened. Our realizing this may make us less apt to feel, and possibly show, disappointment in our ability to support. The client may "hear" us the next day. Even if she does not, our kindness, patience, and good intentions may shine through and affirm her being. Her lack of affirmation from others is probably what created her defense—her foggy thinking, her clouding the issues. She may not believe in herself or in the stability of her outside world enough to feel safe in looking straight at her difficulties. Never underestimate the power of feeling cared for and respected!

Reading Body Language

Much has been written in the helping profession literature about how to tell what is going on with a person by watching her "body language." While I am reasonably familiar with this literature, I do not believe a peer counselor should be overly concerned with this subject. In telephone counseling we obviously cannot observe the client's body language. And in the short time we are with the client face to face, any conclusions based on body language are likely to be out of context. There is much room for error. The client who sits with legs crossed, one leg constantly pumping the air, may be experiencing great tension or may just be a lively, energetic person. The client's facial expression may tell us something about what is going on with her, but with not nearly the accuracy of her words and tone of voice. The client who is drooped like a dying flower, shoulders stooped, head hanging, no direct eye contact, may be depressed—or she may not.

The peer counselor, particularly a beginning one, would do well to focus on other aspects of the peer counseling process and not be too concerned about his or her ability to interpret the client's body language.

Handling Confessionals

Occasionally the peer counselor, particularly a crisis line or telephone counselor, will encounter a client who is feeling remorse and wishes to confess. This type of contact reflects the client's view of morality. She is burdened with guilt and has an urge to tell someone.

Our response to this type of contact may be impacted by our own view of morality. If we have strong moral views, we may have strong feelings when the client confesses. If we feel the client has done something morally wrong, we may feel condemnation. If we feel that what the client says she did was actually not wrong, we may feel an urge to rescue her from her guilt.

In such a call, strong feelings on our part are likely, thus it is doubly important that we be in touch with and in control of our feelings. It is imperative that we come through to the client as nonjudgmental. The client needs a safe place to express her feelings of guilt without being reprimanded. We must not take this moment from her. We must let her deal with the guilt in her own way. We need not fear that she will take our nonjudgmental acceptance of her as approval. If we adhere diligently to our peer counseling skills, she is likely to feel our deep belief in her intrinsic worth and be able to work in her own way toward resolution of her concerns.

At this point, you may be saying, "Well, of course. It's obvious that one should do the same nonjudgmental, open, accepting peer counseling when the client is expressing what she sees, and what we may see, as her immorality. So what's the big deal?"

I have talked with mothers who suffered such rage and frustration that at times they had hurt and almost killed their babies, and were afraid that the next time they would kill them.

I have talked with husbands who had beaten their wives and children, fathers who had sexually abused their children, and men who had raped women and feared doing it again.

Do I abhor their actions? Of course I do. I wanted to yell out to them, "You simply can't do that! We live in a civilized society and what you do is not civilized! How can you be so abusive to others? How can you be so unfair?" I wanted to say these things because people who commit these criminal acts cause me to fear for myself, for the people I love, and for society.

Why did I not speak out against their actions? Why did I not set them straight? There are several reasons. They phoned because they were tormented souls who feared taking violent action against someone if they could not allay their aloneness with their demon. They confessed, and their confession was made more real by having a listener. And I like to believe that whatever likelihood they had of changing their thinking and their behavior was enhanced by their having a nonjudgmental listener. I would have told them to stop doing whatever they were doing if that would have worked. It would not. To have berated them would merely have made them defensive; they had been berated all their lives. I could have explained to them what constitutes acceptable behavior, but they already knew that. Their behaving badly was not a result of their not knowing their behavior was unacceptable. Turning them over to a law enforcement agency was not an option. Confessors do not leave their names and addresses.

In situations such as those described above, the peer counseling methods described in this book undergo their greatest test. In working with a "confessor," our goal of providing an environment that helps a client better know, accept, and love herself is still valid. We cannot be her conscience, and we cannot do her hard work for her. For any human's action to be constructive, she must navigate her own ship. I am not denying that there are humans who behave so destructively that they must be removed from society. But for the peer counselor to make such a decision is neither an option nor an issue. The issue here is how the peer counselor can respond to such a client so as to encourage growth, or, if no growth is possible, to at least avoid causing the client to sink further into her destructive and uncivilized ways.

It goes without saying that if there is even the slightest chance that such a client would consider professional therapy, a referral should be offered.

After a session with a client who is at society's fringe, I admit I am inclined to feel excessive responsibility and to retrace my responses in hopes that I did well. But I fear the truth is that I did not make a big difference one way or another. It took most of a lifetime for the client's personality to develop, and it cannot be fixed in a few minutes. I console myself with the idea that it is good that people like this have a place where they can unburden their souls. After all, this disclosure and self-searching *might* be the beginning of their deciding to change.

Working with Weepers

Getting in touch with the feelings behind her present concerns often causes the client to cry. For us to ignore the tears causes tension for both client and counselor and may cause the former to feel she should not cry. To respond to content at such a time might cause her to feel that her feelings were being ignored. If she cannot talk because of her tears, we might say, "It's all right to cry. I'll just wait until you're ready to talk."

If the client is crying but manages also to keep talking, a nonspecific feeling response is in order.

> "It hurts to think about it."
> or
> "This is hard for you."

Passionate sensitivity in the peer counselor's tone of voice is, in itself, an understanding response. Reflecting detailed and specific feelings, as we do when we are trying to help a client get in touch with her feelings, is not in order here. She already is extremely in touch with her feelings. For example, it is better to avoid:

> "It hurts to think about the night he left you."
> or
> "You are devastated at the death of your child."

Sometimes none of the foregoing efforts works. When the client cries so continuously that she cannot talk, she may be suffering a depression over which she has little control. In such a case, a referral to a professional therapist is in order. But we should use patience and give the session time before giving up and terminating it.

Occasionally, a peer counselor is so moved by a client's story that she or he feels a tear escaping. This is okay. It demonstrates caring involvement. But if we cry so much it gets in the way of our peer counseling, we are probably experiencing emotions stemming from unprocessed feelings of our own. Perhaps the best we can do in this situation is attempt to explain the situation to the client and get another peer counselor to take the case.

Dealing with Silence

The client's reluctance to talk in the beginning of a counseling session (addressed in Chapter 5) probably means something different from her sudden silence well into the session. Initial silences usually mean the client is shy or depressed, or came in or phoned at the suggestion of another and against her will. Silences during the session have a wider range of causes. The client's silence may result from strong feelings about what was just said and her waiting for her feelings to subside, her not feeling understood by the peer counselor and not knowing what to say next, or her unwillingness to trust the peer counselor with her confidences. Or she may be using the silent time to think and absorb what was said previously, particularly if she has just had a new insight. She may be silent as she reviews her concerns before deciding what to say next.

Most inexperienced peer counselors, and many experienced ones, are uncomfortable with silences. Most of us in the business and social world anxiously await the smallest break in conversation so that we can give our own opinion. After all, remaining silent might be interpreted by others as being impolite, distant, or cold, or an indication that we do not have an opinion. Today's society is bent on making every minute count. Silence normally does not count, is not valued very much.

The client's silence during the session presents a real dilemma for the peer counselor. If the client is experiencing strong emotions or is using this time to think, our interrupting the silence might get in her way; however, if she is frightened by strong feelings that have surfaced, our encouraging her to talk about her discomfort may be helpful. The silence may be taking the pressure off her—or putting it on. Such pressure is constructive only if it encourages her to take responsibility for working through her crisis. If the silence disrupts her train of thought to the point that she cannot continue, it is destructive. Often we have no way of knowing if the silence is constructive or destructive. Also, while working on her difficulty is the client's responsibility, it is our responsibility to facilitate; but how can we facilitate if nothing is happening? Our best bet in these circumstances is probably to wait out the silence for a reasonable length of time. This is the client's time, and what she says is her responsibility. A relaxed silence may serve the same purpose as the response "Mm-hm."

I have often suffered what seemed a long silence—silences can seem much longer than they really are—after which the client began talking again, seemingly without having noticed the silence. The client seemed to sense my listening to her silent moments and to be even more encouraged to share her thoughts and feelings.

But eventually, if the client does not terminate the silence, we must act. What was said just prior to the silence may point us toward an appropriate response. Our reflecting or commenting on the content or perceived feelings that preceded the silence is one way to get the session moving again. Here is an example of an appropriate facilitating response when the client was dealing with feelings just prior to the silence.

"You have been silent for awhile. Sometimes when people feel quite strongly about things, it's hard to express it in words. It might help to tell me what you are feeling right now."

Recognizing the cause of her disquiet and being given permission to talk about her present feelings rather than what caused the feelings can be the saving grace that permits the client to continue talking and thus enhance her awareness and growth.

Here are some examples of other facilitating responses.

"A few minutes ago we were talking about. . . . I'm wondering if you find that hard to talk about."

or

"I'm wondering what is causing the silence. If you want time to just think, I'll wait until you want to talk."

If the client appears to be overly tired, or—for whatever reason—seems unwilling or unable to continue with the session, the peer counselor might say: "I sense that you are in a quiet mood. I'm wondering if you may have explored all you wish to today."

Notice that the above responses are neither questions nor suggestions as to what the client should talk about next. That is left up to her. It is particularly important to respond to a silence in an unhurried manner and to keep our tone of voice free from anxiety. The purpose of the response after a silence is to affirm that the silence is noticed and accepted as okay, and to encourage the client to continue if she wishes to do so.

There is always some risk taking on our part when we respond to a silence. Usually we are guessing what caused the silence, and we may guess wrong. The client is usually appreciative of our efforts and will correct us if we are off track. Even a wrong guess and being corrected serves to support a continuing dialogue. A shared silence and a silence that is interrupted in a respectful and affirming way is a warm and special time that has a positive influence on the session.

Being Professional

One does not have to be paid to be professional. Although professionalism is sometimes thought of as being mechanical, cold, or distant, none of these qualities are present in true professionalism. Being professional goes beyond a particular career description, role, or title. It means being competent and efficient; it involves excellence in performance while being oneself.

Being professional means being an expert in a particular field. Although being an expert peer counselor does not mean being an expert in psychotherapy, it does mean knowing peer counseling. It means knowing how to, for example, assess a client's needs, turn a conversation from socializing into a work session, keep the client focused on the session, respond to her appropriately, and terminate the session at the appropriate time. It means knowing one's own limitations and when and how to refer to other professionals and agencies. It means not giving the impression of putting down our co-workers, our agency, or other community agencies and professionals. If our client is critical of others in the helping profession, we can respond so as to confirm that we heard her, being careful that we do not come through as agreeing with her.

Being professional in peer counseling means dressing to the situation, acting in a professional manner, being conscientious and dependable, and being accepting of ourselves when we make mistakes. It means maintaining confidentiality with our client, our co-workers, and our agency.

Confidentiality

Professional therapists have a code of ethics that spells out the confidential nature of the helping relationship. Although such a code may not be set down in writing for the nonprofessional helper, the peer counselor is expected to adhere to confidentiality. (*Confidentiality* is not to be confused with *privileged communication*. The latter refers to the protection of material from disclosure in the courtroom and is addressed in the next section.)

The basic rule of peer counselor confidentiality is that we refrain from telling anyone, including our mate or best friend, the client's name or anything about the client. Knowledge by others of the client's difficulties might be harmful to her and most certainly would prevent her from ever again confiding in us or our agency. But, more important, we either overtly or by implication promised the client confidentiality. We are morally bound to be loyal to this relationship of trust with the client. To break this confidence would destroy the effectiveness of our helping and negatively affect the client's ability to trust. Adherence to confidentiality is the very basis on which the helping relationship exists and succeeds.

It can be tempting to break confidentiality, especially for those of us who normally tend to tell "everything" to our mate or best friend. Our moments with clients sometimes involve living life at its deepest. During a peer counseling session we may experience depths of emotions and insights heretofore unknown to us. Strong feelings do not always end when the session ends. We may come away from our volunteer work in wonder and awe, stunned that a human being can find her- or himself in situations involving such great emotional pain and amazed at their potential for endurance, strength, and growth. It may be hard for us to keep these emotions and insights to ourselves. In addition, many client stories are sensational, and it is attention getting to take center stage and tell a sensational story. Must we really remain silent? Yes! Keeping a confidence is part of being a peer counselor.

The client's name should always be considered confidential. We must not let it be known to anyone outside our agency that a particular individual is a client. Often the client does not want anyone to know she sought help. As a general rule, we should refrain from telephoning a client or returning a telephone call from a client. Someone else may answer the phone and we would be in the awkward position of having to refuse to identify ourself or why we were calling. Also, before phoning another person or agency on the client's behalf, we should obtain the client's permission to use her name.

There are, however, three exceptions to the above. There may be a legitimate need to talk with the agency director or volunteer coordinator about a particular case when we need advice regarding how we should have handled certain aspects of a session or how we should handle similar situations in the future. Also, as will be dealt with in Chapter 10, certain emergency situations may require us to provide co-workers and others with some details of a current client contact. A third possible reason for breaking confidentiality is when a crime is reported and the laws of our state require us to report it. This is discussed in more detail in the next section. Even in these three relatively rare situations, though, we should reveal only the information that our supervisors, co-workers, and others really need to know.

The question sometimes arises as to whether we should promise the client confidentiality. Perhaps the best strategy is to assume confidentiality without raising the issue. If the client should ask specifically if what they tell us will be kept confidential, we can presume that sharing information with other agency personnel on an "as needed" basis or reporting criminal activities as may be required by law will not violate the client's understanding of confidentiality, and we can safely respond to the client by saying, "Yes, what we discuss is confidential."

Observing confidentiality also applies to protecting ourselves, agency staff, and our co-workers. We should never reveal our full name to the client. (Volunteers at crisis lines normally give neither their first nor last name to the client; volunteers of agencies that provide face-to-face peer counseling usually give first names only.) It is crucial that neither home phone numbers nor addresses of peer counselors or staff be given to *anyone*. If they had a phone number, many clients would not hesitate to phone a peer counselor or staff member at home. Also, an occasional hostile client might be dangerous. In my twenty years of volunteering as a peer counselor I have never felt in danger, but there are times when I would have had I not implicitly trusted my co-workers' adherence to confidentiality.

A rather awkward situation arises when a peer counselor happens to see a client in a public place—for example, when walking through a shopping mall. Probably the best way to handle such a situation is, if the client is alone and looks our way, to acknowledge her briefly, not using her name. If she is not alone, it is best not to acknowledge her at all.

Agencies that employ volunteer peer counselors customarily do not keep records about clients except, possibly, nameless statistical information. Peer counselors do not ordinarily take notes when talking with a client face-to-face. If notes are taken, they should be shredded in the client's presence. Many peer counselors routinely take notes when talking with a client over the phone; these should be shredded immediately after the conversation.

The client hands us a gift of trust. We must handle it respectfully and responsibly. The agency we work for is an integral part of our community. It is to our advantage—is our privilege—to honor and uphold our community's integrity.

Legal Implications of Being a Peer Counselor

The question sometimes has been raised regarding whether or not a peer counselor is at risk of legal liability resulting from any claim of loss or injury to the client. Under our legal system, anyone can, of course, file a lawsuit against anyone else for any reason. This is a risk for all of us, whether or not we are a volunteer peer counselor. The risk of our being implicated in a lawsuit pertaining to our work as a peer counselor, however, is quite remote. There are several reasons for this. Peer counselors do not give advice, are not paid for their services, do not hold themselves out to be professional therapists, do not keep records, and serve only clients who have asked for assistance but do not pay for the assistance. These factors provide a powerful legal presumption against any malice or intentional misconduct on the part of the peer counselor or his or her agency.

Another legal issue is whether it ever becomes necessary for peer counselors to breach confidentiality in order to reveal certain information to satisfy legal requirements. Suppose, for example, the client told us of a crime she or someone she knows has committed. This raises several important issues. First, the client may or may not have told us the truth. Some clients are not beyond attempting to get attention by shocking us. Second, our relating what another party told us about herself or a third party would be considered hearsay evidence. We did not actually see the person commit the crime. Also, clients who confide stories of horrors, especially telephone clients, are street smart and highly unlikely to reveal their name or any other information that could lead to their identity. A specific example of when we may be expected to report a crime concerns child abuse. Many states have enacted laws requiring anyone who has knowledge of child abuse to report it. Of consideration here is the legal interpretation of "knowledge." Does hearsay—hearing the client say she is abusing the child, or hearing the child say it has been abused—constitute knowledge, or must we have actually observed evidence of abuse?

While most of the above factors would seem to argue against our reporting a possible criminal activity, the fact remains that to do nothing with such information would seem to many of us to leave our duty as a citizen unfulfilled and possibly to violate the laws of the state in which we reside. Although there is no single simple answer to this dilemma, most volunteer agencies follow several guidelines to minimize the impact on the peer counselor.

First, we should attempt to avoid being placed in a position where breaking confidentiality becomes an issue. If the client begins to tell us that she or someone else has committed a crime, we might remind her that we are not the appropriate agency for dealing with crime. We can offer to provide her with the name and telephone number of an appropriate agency. If she says she doesn't wish to report the supposed crime, we can ask her for permission to report it for her. Although she probably will not provide it, we also should ask for permission to use her name and information on how she may be contacted. If she gives permission to any of these, we are free to report what we know to the proper authorities without violating confidentiality.

If the client is attempting to report to us a case of child abuse, in addition to giving her the name and telephone number of the appropriate social services agency, we might let her know that such agencies ordinarily keep confidential the name of the person reporting child abuse. We should not, however, promise confidentiality on the part of another agency. If confidentiality is important to the client, she can always ask the social worker about this before reporting the abuse. If the caller is a child reporting that he or she has been abused, confidentiality is not an issue. The child has asked for help and, presumably, has provided identifying information. No harm can be done by our passing this information on to the appropriate authorities.

If, in spite of our best efforts to avoid being placed in such a position, a seemingly reliable client does tell us of a possible criminal activity, our best course of action is to pass the responsibility on to professionals or paid staff in our agency. The peer counselor is no more expected to be an interpreter of the law than is any other citizen. We do not practice law or law enforcement. For this reason, most volunteer peer counseling agencies have an attorney either on staff or available on a consulting basis. Since the attorney would be knowledgeable about the laws in his or her state, and also would be in a position to evaluate the information concerning the particular case, the final decision would be his or hers. In the absence of an attorney with responsibility for advising about such issues, the employed staff of the volunteer agency should be in a position to advise us regarding what action, if any, we should take.

Is the peer counselor working in an environment where there is imminent danger of a wrong decision placing him or her in jeopardy of a lawsuit, prosecution for a crime, or being called as a witness in a criminal case? Fortunately, no. In my twenty years of peer counseling, I have never been required to defend myself or testify in a court of law concerning my peer counseling activities, nor have I ever heard of a volunteer who has.

9

Telephone Counseling

Telephone counseling is similar to face-to-face counseling in that we begin the session, respond to content, reflect feelings, occasionally assist a client in exploring options and making decisions, and end the session as described in Chapters 2 through 6. However, peer counseling in the two settings also differs in significant ways that have profound implications for both the peer counselor and the client.

In telephone peer counseling we have no visual communication clues; for example, we cannot observe the client's facial expression, gestures, and body posture. We may not know if he is laughing or crying. We do not know if his gestures agree with or contradict his words. We have only limited control of the setting. We are partially in his world but we cannot see his world. We do not know if he is calling from his home, work, automobile, a pay phone, a jail, the golf course, or a mental hospital. We may hear a glass clinking but not know what he is drinking. We may hear loud background noises but not know if it is a radio, television, or other people. We do not know if he called of his own accord or if he has someone hovering over and prompting him.

The client can see neither our facial expression nor our nodding our head to indicate that we have heard him. He must depend entirely on our verbal "continuers" and other responses. He is more likely to misinterpret or misunderstand what we say. The warmth of human contact is somewhat reduced for him and he may be distracted by elements of his environment. Also, he may feel emboldened by his anonymity and feel less threatened in his familiar surroundings.

This chapter addresses those aspects of peer counseling that are unique to telephone counseling.

Peer Counselor Rights

Peer counselors have a right to insist on an environment that is suitable for a private conversation. If any background noises are unbearably distracting, we might say:

> "I am having a great deal of trouble hearing you. Would you turn your television down. I will wait."

Or if the client is calling from his car phone, we might say:

> "I can't hear you well enough to make out what you are saying. Would you phone back when conditions are more favorable?"

In telephone peer counseling we need also to be aware of background noises on our end of the line. We may have to "shush" our co-workers.

Some clients will offer their phone number and ask the peer counselor to phone them back or insist that the peer counselor they talked with on their last call phone them back. We should never phone the client (except possibly in an emergency situation). Here are some reasons for this. If we phone the client, someone other than the client may answer the phone. If that person insists on knowing who is phoning, we are put in the position of betraying a confidentiality the client had a right to expect. Or we may phone the client's number several times and not be able to reach him, leaving him feeling we broke our promise. The phones may be busy at the volunteer agency right up to our scheduled time to leave, and we may never have a chance to phone him back. Or we may phone him back and he may not be in the mood to talk. What earlier seemed like a life or death event may now be very low priority for him. When the client asks us to phone him back, we need only explain that the agency has a policy against this but that he may phone anytime he wishes.

During a telephone peer counseling session, a client sometimes will ask the peer counselor to "hang on." In addition to being preempted by "call waiting," clients have asked me to hang on while they "feed the dog," "take clothes out of the dryer," or "change the baby." Each peer counselor must use his or her own discretion regarding being willing to be put on hold; in general, the best rule is "don't!" The client can be told—and quickly of course, before he is gone—that we cannot wait, but that he can phone back later.

Silences on the Telephone

How the peer counselor can deal with the client's being silent in the beginning of the session was covered in Chapter 5. The client's becoming silent at times during the session was discussed in Chapter 8. However, there are some special considerations in responding to silence during telephone counseling.

Ideally, silences should not be as long on the phone as they may be in face-to-face peer counseling. However, ending the silence does not necessitate our taking charge of the call. Following are examples of statements a peer counselor might make to end the silence while leaving the responsibility for the call with the client.

When the client is silent, we do not know if he is still there. And if we are silent, he does not know if we are still there. We can assure him:

> "I'm here, I'm listening."
>   or
> "I'm still here. Are you still there?"

We may need to check out what is going on in the client's world. For example:

"I'm hearing some background noises and wonder if there is someone with you and if, perhaps, you are not free to say what you want to say."

or

"It sounds as if you are crying."

or

"I can't tell if you're laughing or crying."

If we hear whispering, we might say:

"I notice some whispering going on in the background and I'm wondering if you really want to talk with me right now. I'm happy to talk with you, but only if you really want to talk."

The Defensive Caller

Occasionally a peer counselor encounters a caller who is constantly and consistently on the defensive.

CLYDE: Everything has gone wrong for me. I lost my job. My wife left me. Nothing I do turns out right.

PEER C: It seems to you that everything has gone wrong. You lost your job, and your wife left you.

CLYDE: Well, no, she didn't exactly leave me. She just went to stay at her mother's for a while. But I'm pretty sure she will leave soon and stay gone.

PEER C: You believe she will soon end the marriage.

CLYDE: No, she wouldn't do that. She just wants me to think she's going to divorce me. She keeps saying I had rather just hang out than find a job.

PEER C: She's upset that you don't have a job.

CLYDE: Oh, I have a job. I've been there fifteen years. They wouldn't dare fire me. It's just that there's no work to do right now. The company is downsizing.

PEER C: The company is downsizing, but you didn't lose your job.

CLYDE: Well, not really. They . . .

If the above client is a new volunteer's first client, he or she, under-standably, might start screaming at this point. While I have done exactly that, there is a better way.

One strategy when encountering defensive clients is to refrain from responding to the content or reflecting perceived feelings and simply to continue saying, "Mm-hm." Possibly, after getting further into his story, he will trust more and not need to be so defensive. But don't bet on it. His defensive front is probably an established lifestyle. Another strategy is to confront him with his contradictions. I tried this once. It went this way.

PEER C: I notice that when I respond to what you say, you seem to contradict yourself. I wonder why that is.

CLYDE: I don't contradict myself!

Oh well, I tried. Attempting to refer the client to a professional therapist could be in order here. But the chances of success are slim. Probably the only practical resolution is to terminate the call.

PEER C: I'm sorry but I am a peer counselor and my training is lim-ited. I am not going to be able to help you. I will be glad to refer you to a professional therapist if you wish.

CLYDE: I don't like being told that I'm crazy and need a shrink. You could help me if you would.

PEER C: I'm going to have to hang up now. Goodbye.

The defensive caller may be trying to get attention and con-trol. Staying on the line with him would only contribute to this self-defeating lifestyle.

Sexual Calls

Yes! Crisis lines do get obscene phone calls. Although female peer counselors are the usual targets, male peer counselors are not immune. The rule is to treat these obscene calls just as we would at home—as soon as the call is recognized as obscene, simply hang up without speaking. But often it is not this simple. The telephone is a good maneuvering tool. Some callers are clever, imaginative, and very good actors. These obscene calls often start out very much like legitimate calls about sexual concerns.

One clue that the caller phoned for the sole purpose of using the peer counselor in his pursuit of sexual gratification is a beginning statement pretending undue modesty. For example,

"This is kind of embarrassing, and I don't know how to say it."
or
"Are you sure it is okay for me to say anything I want to?"
or
"You are a woman, maybe you can give me a woman's point of view concerning what happened to me."

A clue that the caller may be masturbating is his heavy and erratic breathing. However, this clue alone is not sufficient to treat the call as obscene. Heavy, erratic breathing can also be caused by certain physical afflictions. Another hint that the call is not legitimate is when the caller asks personal questions, such as "Are you married?" or "What do you look like?" An appropriate peer counselor response is, "Tell me why you phoned." Most sexual callers hang up at this point. If he continues talking, he may attempt to make his story a little more plausible in an effort to manipulate the peer counselor into talking. If this does not happen, he may get more graphic, thinking this will at least cause her to verbally protest. These callers' sole purpose in phoning seems to be to hear the female talk. If this does not happen, the call does not serve its purpose. The peer counselor's objective in what seems to be an obscene call is to talk as little as possible while giving the caller the benefit of the doubt until evidence indicates otherwise. As soon as the counselor suspects the call to be inappropriate, she can quit responding to content and feelings and instead limit her responses to an occasional "Mm-hm." As soon as it becomes obvious that the call is inappropriate, she can say, "I'm convinced nothing constructive is happening here, so I am going to hang up," and do so.

Crisis lines also frequently get calls from transvestites (cross-dressers). These callers most often are males who may or may not be homosexual. Care must be taken not to label all calls from transvestites as "obscene." Many transvestites have very real concerns and may be genuine in their call for help. For example, he may have just been "discovered" by his mate or a co-worker, and the discoverer may be totally unable to relate to the transvestite's obsessions.

But if such a caller insists on describing, in detail, the outfit he has on or the one he wore to a party recently, we can safely assume he gets more sexual gratification from his cross-dressing when he has a listener. While his language is unlikely to be obscene, his use of the crisis line to satisfy his sexual desires is inappropriate. We should tell him so, but gently. This type of caller usually seems sensitive and apologizes for being inappropriate.

Another type of sexual caller who frequently calls crisis lines is the fantasizer. (All of the sexual fantasizers I have encountered as a peer counselor have been males.) This fantasizer is most imaginative. He is often young and convincing enough to make it difficult for us to tell whether his story is fact or fiction. The fantasizer may tell about how he unintentionally observed a female member of his family (or his sister's girlfriend) in some state of undress. He may ask if this is wrong. He may say that his mother, or aunt, enticed him into a sexual relationship, and that he is worried about it.

What typically identifies such a caller as a fantasizer is his language. While it may not be obscene, it usually becomes graphic. If the counselor requests that he tell his story without getting graphic, he usually loses interest and hangs up.

It is unfortunate that the anonymity afforded by crisis lines is attractive to such callers. But it is, and we must make the best of it. While knowing some of the characteristics of sexual calls may help us to recognize them, even experienced peer counselors get taken in. When we graciously give our time, attention, and caring only to discover the caller is using us for his own sexual gratification, we feel, we *are*, exploited and molested. After such a call, most peer counselors find it helpful to take a break from the phones, draft another peer counselor or staff member to listen, and talk out their feelings.

Although the obscene caller is a major concern because his calls are so personally intrusive, they are fortunately a very low percentage of the total calls. Most calls are a rewarding experience.

The Abusive Caller

Now and then a caller is downright abusive. He will shout, curse, and complain about getting a busy signal when he tried to call. He may tell us we aren't helping and that we don't care about him. Obviously there is no reason to stay on the line with such a caller— though I do give it one try.

PEER C: If you would like to calm down and tell me what is really wrong, I can talk with you.

This usually makes the client even more emotional.

ROY: I'm *telling* you what's wrong, and you won't listen!

PEER C: I am going to hang up now. You may phone back if you really have something you wish to work on. Goodbye.

Usually this last statement is said while the client is ranting. He no doubt gets payback from putting people down, but not a healthy payback. The best we can do for him is to refuse to be his victim.

The Prank Caller

Crisis lines get their share of prank calls: calls from persons who are pretending they have a problem and need help. Many of these calls are from teenagers or children. Some are from adults. I believe one's intuition is the best guide for detecting that the call is concocted. When we take such a call, something just doesn't feel right. I suppose it is the caller's tone of voice—his insincerity. One way of getting more information about these suspect calls is to wait longer than usual to respond and then respond with "Mm-hm"s, essentially letting the caller do most of the talking. A prankster gets very uncomfortable doing the talking. An adult prankster either hangs up quickly or becomes abusive; a playful teenager often starts giggling and then hangs up.

An adult who uses the telephone this way seems to be bitter and perhaps shy. He seems to be using the telephone as a weapon, as a way of having some control over another person. When this type of caller becomes aware that we are not deceived, he sometimes becomes extremely angry and abusive, hanging up abruptly. He then will phone back—again, and again, and again—giving another name and sometimes trying to disguise his voice. A lecture on "tying up the line when people with real problems are trying to get through" generally has no effect whatsoever on an apprehended prankster, and *we* are tying up the line while we sermonize. Chances are that the prankster will not even stay on the line long enough to listen. One way, and probably the best, to resolve this dilemma is to leave the phone off the hook for a few minutes. He is easily distracted.

When my intuition tells me the call is a prank but I am not sure, I choose to err on the side of remaining vulnerable. In such a case I would rather be taken advantage of than take advantage of.

The Unintelligible Call

Consider the following dialogue:

PEER C: Hello. This is the Women's Center.

JUDITH: He said he was coming, but he is not here yet. What do you think I should do when he says he is coming but he doesn't? Tell me, what should I do?

PEER C: Perhaps if you could tell me a little more about your situation we could work together on it.

JUDITH: Well, what is there to say? This is the right day, isn't it? I thought it was the right day. My other son went on vacation. He won't be back for days.

Occasionally an unintelligible call is from a caller who talked, earlier in the day, to some other peer counselor, and he mistakes us for her or him. We can check this out: "Have you talked with someone here earlier today?" Generally, though, a caller who has phoned previously begins by asking, "Are you the one I talked with earlier today?" Muddled speaking more likely is from someone who is mentally handicapped or under the influence of alcohol or drugs. There is little we can do with this type of phone call except, perhaps, hit it a glancing blow by making guesses and asking questions to see if we can make enough sense of it to be helpful.

PEER C: Who is it that said he was coming and isn't here yet?

JUDITH: Like I told you, my son!

PEER C: Could you phone him to see why he hasn't come?

JUDITH: Okay. I'll phone him. I do hope this is the right day. [How to deal with the mentally handicapped or substance impaired is addressed further in the next chapter.]

The Repeat Caller

Though callers to crisis lines are not asked to give their name and rarely do, some phone so frequently that they can be readily identified by most of the volunteers. (When there is a constructive reason for doing so, volunteer peer counselors do talk to each other about their calls.) For example, the woman who always talks about her dogs may be called the "dog woman," the woman who cares for her elderly parents may be called "the caregiver," and the homebound, handicapped man may be referred to as "the wheelchair man." Many of these repeat callers suffer either a mental or physical handicap. It is often difficult to determine whether talking with them helps or hurts them. A crisis line is not set up for continuing relationships with callers. On the other hand, some of these callers have no one else to talk to.

Some agencies handle this awkward situation by keeping a record of the calls—the time and the content. A group of staff, volunteers, and a professional therapist consultant evaluates each repeat caller, develops a plan, and advises the peer counselors how to handle each subsequent call from the individual. An evaluation often results in the caller's being allowed a certain amount of phone time. Other callers may be asked, as tactfully as possible, not to phone again. Although asking a client to stop calling may not deter him initially, repeating the message every time he calls eventually brings the desired results.

The guidelines for counseling with a repeat caller who is allowed limited calls is the same as for any other caller except that he is allowed to talk for longer periods of time without a playback. Since the repeat caller is not in a growth mode, the focus is more on meeting his temporary need, which often is simply to be able to tell someone about his day. To help him focus it sometimes helps to ask him what prompted him to phone at that particular time. A few of the clients who are given limits on how long they can talk follow these directions to the minute and close their call themselves, but generally the peer counselor must keep an eye on the clock and assertively close the call by saying, for example, "Our time is up for today. You may phone back tomorrow if you wish."

If firm steps are not taken with repeat callers, peer counselors spend most of their time with a relatively small group of individuals.

Ending the Telephone Session

Guidelines for effecting a smooth ending to a telephone peer counseling session are the same as ending a face-to-face session, the object being to bring a gradual and steady closure to the conversation. After some time, and when we sense that about all has been done that can be done in one telephone conversation, we can say:

> "We have just a few more minutes. Is there anything you wish to say before we end?"

Often, conditions do not permit a telephone peer counseling session an ideal closing. For example, during a session, a client may begin whispering or abruptly change the subject. This happens often when clients phone from work. At such times we can check out the reason.

PEER C: I notice you are whispering [or that you suddenly changed the subject]. I am wondering if someone came in and you need to hang up.

ALICE: Yes.

PEER C: I understand. Feel free to phone back any time you wish. You may not be able to reach me next time, but there is always a peer counselor here who can talk with you.

ALICE: Goodbye.

Even with our attempts to bring some form of closure before hanging up the phone, telephone peer counseling sessions often suffer an abrupt ending. Other than our making sure the call does not run over forty or fifty minutes, there is no firm prescheduled ending time. So for forty or fifty minutes, as long as the session seems productive, we remain in a "continue" mode. On the other hand, the client often does not think about ending the conversation until, for example, he suddenly realizes it is time to go to work, or he hears his wife enter the house. Suddenly he says, "Gotta go," and hangs up, leaving us with our mouth half-open. We never know what really happened. Being a peer counselor means placing ourselves in a vulnerable position. Protecting ourselves from this vulnerability would require too great a price. Our caution would keep us from really being there for the client. At times like these a great deal of flexibility and a sense of humor help.

Summing Up

If this chapter leaves you with a rather hopeless feeling about whether telephone peer counseling results in anything positive, it is probably because the atypical call is given more space here than the typical call. The reason for this is that you already have learned the skills to handle the typical call (the basic peer counseling skills covered in previous chapters). Telephone peer counseling is convenient for both client and peer counselor, and when adjustments are made to accommodate the lack of visual cues and the unique assortment of callers, it can be remarkably effective and rewarding.

10

Special Cases

So far, the information in this book has focused on peer counseling skills that can be used to benefit most clients, no matter what their concern. Most clients, whether their concern is divorce, unemployment, parenting, or interpersonal relationships, have the same emptiness, the same frailty of self, and the same lack of emotional nourishment. The primary need of most clients then is to better know, accept, and love themselves. The primary goal of the peer counselor in working with these clients is to provide an atmosphere conducive to meeting that need, and the focus of the previous chapters is on the skills needed to meet this primary goal.

This chapter is different in that the focus is on three categories of clients who have certain characteristics in common and whose needs differ considerably from those of the typical client. While the individuals in these three categories also have a need to better know, accept, and love themselves, they have other needs that override the more elemental one. It is these overriding needs, and the skills needed to meet these needs, that are addressed here.

For clients in the first category of "special cases," those in emergency situations, the overriding need of the moment is for physical survival and well-being. For clients in the second category, those whose thinking is impaired, the overriding need that a peer counselor can address is to cope with their immediate emotional pain. For those in the third category, the terminally ill, the overriding need is to come to terms with and accept their own imminent death.

Upon first contact with any client, we should begin by using the basic peer counseling skills discussed in previous chapters. However, once we begin receiving clues that the client fits one of these "special cases" categories, we should use the specialized skills addressed here.

An Introduction to Emergency Situations

As is noted above, one category of special cases is clients who are in emergency situations, that is, who are facing an imminent threat to their physical survival or well-being. This may include, but is not restricted to, the suicidal, the physically abused, the homeless, the runaway teenager, and the client suffering from a reaction to drugs. In the following sections, identifying and dealing with the suicidal client is discussed first, primarily because reasonably standard specific guidelines have been established for working with this type of client. Other types of emergency situations on the other hand are so varied that only very general guidelines can be provided. These are presented later. Because the peer counselor's contact with emergency situations (with the possible exception of the homeless) is primarily by telephone, the information about emergency situations assumes telephone communication.

Identifying the Suicidal Client

Rarely if ever does a peer counselor pick up the crisis line phone and hear a client say, "I am going to kill myself." The client's desperate cry for help usually is nowhere near that straightforward. For this reason we should begin every call, even the ones that turn out to be from a suicidal client, by responding to the content of what the client says. During the session we must be alert to anything the client says that could even remotely be interpreted to mean that she plans to kill herself. Examples of phrases that may alert us to such a possibility are:

"Life is empty."
"I have lost hope."
"Life is no good."
"I'm not of any use to anyone."
"There's nothing I can do to change my life for the better."
"Life has no meaning."
"My family would be better off with me not around."
"I just can't go on this way much longer."
"There is nothing to live for."
"I'd be better off dead."
"All my problems will soon be over."
"It won't matter after Monday."

Some other evidence that she may be suicidal are:

- Her stating that she is suffering from depression, especially that she has been depressed for a long time
- Indications of alcohol or drug abuse
- A history of attempting suicide
- Existence of a chronic debilitating physical illness
- Extreme passivity or extreme hostility
- Indications that she has no friends
- Indications that she has no passion in life
- Indications of being under severe stress.

If we become suspicious that our client may be suicidal, we should check it out by asking her, in a straightforward manner: "Are you thinking about suicide?"

If she is not suicidal, she will tell us so. Asking will not cause her to become suicidal. If she wants to know why we ask, we can simply repeat to her what she said that caused us to wonder. If she says she does plan to kill herself, we need to switch immediately to emergency mode. We are no longer attempting to help the client grow; we are trying to help save her life.

It may be difficult for us to realize this potential suicide is for real. The suicidal client does not always sound as we would expect someone in a life or death situation to sound. In fact, in her attempt to escape her pain, she may not realize the full impact of the step she is contemplating—but we must. If we do, it may be that our tone of voice, which reflects the gravity of this potential tragedy, will be the first thing that communicates to her the reality of what she is proposing. Also, we need to see the reality of the situation so we can gather the essential information and give the required instructions.

Gathering Additional Information from the Suicidal Client

Although considerable details are provided below for dealing with the suicidal client, these can be summarized into two possible courses of action. We can:

1. Help the client formulate a plan of action for protecting herself physically by assisting her in stabilizing her emotions, realizing reality, and gaining perspective. (In other words, assist the client in thinking rationally at a time when her elevated emotions cause her to be disorganized, confused, and overwhelmed.)
2. When needed and appropriate, telephone another person or agency to come to her assistance.

These are the only options available to us. We can neither go get her and take her to the hospital if she is injured nor make her safe by taking the gun or the pills away from her. And we must be careful not to attempt to practice law or medicine. We will be more composed, and our efforts will be more focused, if we realize these limitations.

Even with our limitations, however, we can be a great deal of help to a suicidal client, even instrumental in saving her life. Though we now have shifted into emergency mode, which requires taking charge, being directive, asking questions, and giving instructions, our first responsibility is to attempt to show our respect for the client's ambivalent feelings of wanting to die and wanting to live. (She says she wants to die but her phoning us indicates she wants to live.) The suicidal client needs desperately to know we care. And we need information and cooperation from her. We will get neither if she perceives us to be a cold, methodical interrogator. Thus our first step in dealing with a suicidal client is to build a relationship, to relate as one person to another. Sometimes we have plenty of time to accomplish this—sometimes it needs to happen quickly. Our second question to her will be: "Have you already harmed yourself?"

When dealing with a client who has already hurt herself, time is of the essence, so we will have to work on building a relationship while simultaneously taking the following actions, in the following order.

- Get her address, including apartment number. We should tell her we need her address in case we need to phone for help.
- Learn the specifics about what she has done to harm herself so we can assess the nature, degree, and immediacy of the danger.
- Learn where the means she used (e.g., gun, razor, pills) are located. Learn if the gun is loaded.
- Get her name and telephone number.
- Phone for emergency help if needed.

The reason for the particular order of these actions is that we are attempting to gather information in its order of criticality in case she becomes unable to talk with us. We need to have a notepad and pencil readily available so that we can keep careful notes of the critical information.

Getting the needed information in a kind, caring, but authoritative tone of voice within the possible time limitations is quite a challenge. Well, actually, it is more akin to walking a tightrope. But it is doable.

If she resists giving us identifying information, we should not push. However, as we talk with her, we should periodically repeat the request. We should also be alert to the possibility of her providing some identifying information, either intentionally or unintentionally, without its being labeled as such.

To assess the nature, degree, and immediacy of the danger, we must try to learn what she has done to harm herself and what is going on with her and how she feels *right now*. We need to sound kind but authoritative. We need specific details: Is she in pain? Does she feel sleepy? What kind of medication did she take, what strength, how much did she take, and when did she take it? Where is the gun now? Is it loaded? What did she cut herself with, and on what part of her body? Where is the weapon now? It takes very little time to gather this information, and having it is critical to our knowing how to proceed.

Once we have the needed information, we must judge how great, and how imminent, is the danger. If we judge that her injuries could cause death soon, we should phone for assistance. We should tell her we are going to do so; should she ask us not to, we should disregard her request. She has given us information that indicates that she is in imminent danger of dying and information identifying her location. And she did this knowing why we wanted the information. This constitutes permission. If she becomes unable to talk with us, we will consider her phoning us as permission to use identifying information she intentionally or unintentionally gave us.

If we have a second telephone line available, we should phone Emergency Services or another appropriate agency on the second line, keeping her on the phone. It is all right if she hears the call.

We should tell Emergency Services that a serious threat of suicide has been made, and that the person has already harmed herself. We need to give Emergency Services all the details: address (including the apartment number); the name of the client; how she has harmed herself, including, for example, the type and amount of medication. If there is a weapon, we should be certain to tell them what it is and where it is. If it is a gun, we must tell them whether it is loaded.

If we do not have a second telephone line, we will have to tell the client we are going to hang up to phone for help, and that we will call her right back (after being sure we have her correct phone number).

After phoning for help, our next job is to have the client unlock her door if she is able, and come back to the phone after doing so. Her unlocking the door is important. She may not be able to later. We should emphasize that we will wait and that she is not to hang up the phone.

Then we should talk with the client until Emergency Services arrives, keeping her as calm as possible, assuring her that help is on the way. When help arrives, we will ask to speak with them. Only after we confirm that appropriate assistance is there is our job over. Then we can take a deep breath, try to relax, and get ready for the next phone call.

Now let us back up a bit and assume the client has *not* harmed herself. After she has told us that "yes," she is suicidal, but "no," she has not yet harmed herself, our next question to her is: "Have you planned how you would commit suicide?"

She might say, for example:

> "Well, no, not really, it's just that life is so hard sometimes that I've thought of suicide. I don't think I could really do it, but sometimes I think of it as a way out."

A client who says this is really distressed and needs our care, which can be exhibited by our regular peer counseling skills. But we probably do not have an emergency on our hands.

Suppose, though, that the client answers, "Yes, I do have a plan."

Although we have more time, our first responsibility to her is the same as for the client who has already harmed herself: to attempt to show our respect for her ambivalent feelings of wanting to die and wanting to live. We can do this by talking in a soft, sober, and caring manner as we further assess the seriousness and immediacy of danger in the situation. Our next question is: "What do you plan to do?"

If her plan sounds like something that might succeed in killing or seriously injuring her, we need to learn whether she has readily available the tools that she plans to use. As applicable, we can ask questions such as:

> "Do you have a gun? Where is the gun now?"
> "Do you already have that medication? Where is it now?"
> "Do you have a razor? Where is it now?"
> "Are you on the twentieth floor of the building right now?"

If she has the means at hand to harm herself, we need to learn the deadliness of her chosen method, how dangerous her tools are. We will ask her, for example:

> "Is the gun loaded?"
> "How many pills do you have? What strength?"
> "Which floor are you on now?"

If our client is in imminent danger, our next job is to help her decrease the danger, to persuade her to dispose of or make the means less available. If she has a gun aimed at her head, we will gently try to persuade her to put the gun in a drawer or on top of the refrigerator, some place less available; or we will try to get her to flush the pills, or at least put them in the back of a drawer. We can tell her it is very difficult for us to talk with her while we know the means are there in front of her. If she shows resistance, we will continue to talk with her in a soft voice and try again a bit later. Our next question to her is: "Are you alone? Who is with you? Where are they right now? Can they help you?"

By asking if anyone is with her, we may learn if she has a close friend or relative who cares about her, and whether or not we can count on that person to help. After we talk with the client awhile, we may need to talk with that person. Or it might be that the person with the client is the target of her hostility. That person might even be in danger from her. The answers to these questions will impact what we say to the client as well as whether or not we will phone for help.

The client's mood and attitude may prevent our going quickly and directly down the line in asking the questions given above. Though our focus remains on gathering needed information, we should take whatever time is necessary to attempt to relate to the client and build trust. But we will return to the questions as quickly as we reasonably can. Each time she resists giving us the information, we will defer that approach only to return to it, again and again, undauntedly and without defensiveness.

Further Dealing with the Suicidal Client

Based on the information we have obtained in response to the above questions (and on how successful we have been in getting the client to make the means of suicide less available), we will judge how much danger she is in and how immediate it is. Although our further efforts will be similar in many ways regardless of our perception of the seriousness of the situation, our focus will be somewhat different. For the client who is in a high state of danger, our focus will be more on getting help to her. For the client who seems not to be in imminent danger, our focus will lean more toward helping her stabilize her emotions and handle her panic herself. In either case, continuing to attempt to establish trust is critical.

By our intense listening, sober tone of voice, and use of continuers, we can let the client know we hear her story and accept the seriousness of her situation. She needs to share—to get away from the isolation of her concern—and we need to know enough about her situation to act wisely in guiding her. Going too fast does not work. We need to respond to the content of what she says, not in detail, but in brief summaries so as to let her know we heard while not encouraging her to dwell too long on her story. Her prolonged focus on the details might increase the pessimism that causes her to be suicidal. At the same time, however, we should refrain from discouraging her from talking. After all, as long as she is talking, we know she is still alive. Also, her talking will help alleviate her stress, and our listening will help build her trust in us.

With kindness and caring, we should allow her to express her feelings. We should respond in generalities to the content of what she says she feels. We can let her know we hear her pain and that we know she feels awful. We should not, however, reflect detailed specifics of feelings we perceive her to be feeling. This is not the time to encourage her to get more deeply in touch with her assorted feelings. We can let her know that we hear her ambivalent feelings, that something terrible is going on to cause her to want to end her life, yet that part of her desires to live. Our seeming not to understand her wishes to die would cause her to feel misunderstood.

The suicidal client may indicate that she feels little and worthless. If so, we can affirm her with statements such as: "I am glad you phoned us. It took courage for you to do that."

On the other hand, the client may be angry and defiant. (It has been said that suicide is the ultimate temper tantrum—a permanent solution to a temporary problem.) She may see the present situation as her last effort to control. We should not argue with her and thus create a power struggle.

After talking with the client for a while, we will have gained some understanding of the beliefs and emotions that hold terror for her and that she is attempting to escape. And we can hope she will have gained sufficient control over them to be able to consider our suggestions. But in our appeal to her to delay or abort her plan to commit suicide, we need to keep in mind that, while *our* primary goal is to assist her in getting out of physical danger, *her* primary goal is to escape emotional pain. Therefore, we will not try to talk her out of killing herself, but instead will present viable alternatives to help her cope with her feelings of helplessness and hopelessness. She may not be aware of the resources available to her. Some examples of what we might suggest are:

> "It really does help to talk with a therapist. I will help you find a suitable one."
>
> "If you can't afford a therapist, I will help you get an appointment at the mental health clinic."
>
> "You may phone us as often as you like to talk with us about your concerns."
>
> "There are many medications on the market now that lift depression. Your therapist or physician can help you." (Some clients refuse to go to a therapist but will readily go to their physician.)
>
> "Often career counselors can be a great help in finding a job."
>
> "I know of a support group you can join that would help alleviate your loneliness."
>
> "Home care is now available for your elderly mother; this would give you some relief. I will help you find this resource."

If her thinking seems to be sufficiently positive for her to accept and show intent to follow up on some of our suggested alternatives, we need to provide whatever assistance we can in helping her to make appointments or to take other appropriate action.

This may be all that is needed. If we judge that she needs additional, immediate support, however, we can attempt to phone for help or encourage her to phone for help.

We can say, "I'm thinking at this point that we need to get in touch with someone who can be supportive of you until you can get to the therapist [or whatever action has been agreed upon]. Can you think of a relative or friend who might be willing to come stay with you, or at least keep in close touch?"

Our first attempts in getting help should be to get the client's relatives or friends. It is better if she will agree to ask them for the help she needs. Often, though, she will be hesitant about asking for help. After we are sure we have the client's consent, it is permissible for us to phone them. We need to tell them what agency we are with, the client's name, and that she is suicidal and needs some support until she can take the next step in dealing with her difficulties.

If the client says she does not have any relatives or friends she can call on, and if we judge it is not safe for her to stay by herself, we need to get her permission to phone Emergency Services to take her to the hospital. When a person has not yet injured herself, deciding whether or not to phone for assistance is a delicate matter. We do not want our agency to gain the reputation of phoning Emergency Services or other agencies unnecessarily. But we do not want to leave her in danger. She may, for example, have refused to make less available or disposed of the means of suicide, or she may still be very depressed or agitated.

Often, if we pursue it longer, and if the client realizes that her alternative is to have Emergency Services take her to a hospital, she will think of a friend she can phone or have us phone. If not, we want to use good judgment, but if undecided about what to do, we should err on the side of phoning Emergency Services. After all, a life is at stake. We will try, however, to get the client's permission before we do. If she will not give it but has given us her name and address, we may decide to phone anyway, depending on how critical we judge the situation to be. If we do, we should be honest and tell her we are going to do so.

If the client will not consider our getting help for her, and our decision is not to go over her head, we can make one last attempt before we hang up to influence her to get rid of the means: to flush the pills, or unload the gun and put it way back in the closet and put the bullets in another room. If we are successful, we can wait while she does this. We can bargain with her for time by working out an agreement with her. For example, we can challenge her to agree that she will not commit suicide until she sees a therapist, or that if she feels this way again, she will phone us or commit herself to a hospital. Then we can attempt to work with her in planning how she will use the time until she can get help.

Leaving the client at this point may seem like a rather pathetic ending to high drama. We have poured our adrenaline, heart, soul, and especially our mind into trying to help her. And for it to end like this? But there can be no truly satisfactory ending to this story, certainly not immediately. We will probably never know what happened next. This can leave us feeling incomplete as well as exhausted and emotionally drained.

These are the cases we tend to go over and over in our minds, reconsidering whether we said and did the right things. Chances are we were far from perfect. But we do need to be fair with ourselves. The client's difficulties began long before this hour. We are responsible for neither her difficulties nor her solutions. Also, people who truly want to kill themselves will do so—if not today, eventually. That is their right. Chances are, what we said and did are not as critical as whether or not we were truly warm and caring.

Examples of Dealing with the Suicidal Client

Working with the suicidal client is usually a long, slow, tedious process. The following examples are of necessity greatly abbreviated. The first example is of a suicidal phone call to a crisis line from a middle-aged male.

PEER C: Hello. This is the crisis line.

DON: Can you talk to me?

PEER C: Yes, I can.

DON: I'm feeling really down. My wife packed her things and left last night. We've been having trouble, but I didn't know it was this bad. She left me for another man. I guess that's what hurts so bad.

PEER C: Your wife's leaving with another man leaves you hurting.

(*Client talks for ten minutes or so, going into detail about the problems in their marriage, repeating that he did not know it was this bad. He continues.*)

DON: She was my whole life. I love her so. Without her, I don't want to go on. I'm nothing without her. Life is meaningless. I'll be better off dead. I just can't stand this much pain.

PEER C: I can tell you're really hurting. Are you saying you are thinking of suicide?

DON: Yes. I can't go on this way.

PEER C: Do you have a plan to kill yourself?

DON: Yes, I'm going to shoot myself and get it over with fast. Anything just to quit hurting so bad.

PEER C: Do you have a gun?

DON: Yeah, it's right here and it's loaded. I just thought I would talk to somebody first. But it's no use. I just can't go on.

PEER C: I know you are really, really hurting right now. I understand your wish to get out of your pain. But I hope you will let me help. I care about you. Together, I really believe we can work out some ways you won't hurt so much.

Don: I don't see how. She's not going to come back.

Peer C: After we talk, I believe you may begin to see some ways you can cope and not hurt so much. But you know, I am very uncomfortable knowing you have that gun there. What room are you in right now?

Don: I'm in the kitchen.

Peer C: Would you do this for me? Would you put the gun on top of the refrigerator while we talk?

Don: Talking won't help.

Peer C: Maybe not. But then it might. What do you have to lose? You can always shoot yourself later. But if you do it now, there might have been a way and you would never find out. Just put it on top of the refrigerator, and then come back to the phone. I'll wait for you.

Notice that the peer counselor did not contradict the client outright when he said, "Talking won't help." Neither did he or she tell the client he should not shoot himself, but rather allowed him to save face by suggesting he wait until later. Suicidal clients do not take kindly to being told they are wrong. As the client's emotions had subsided a bit, the peer counselor did insist on a reasonable atmosphere for their talking. Having learned, however, that he was not eager to cooperate in putting the gun away, the peer counselor did not *ask* him a second time if he would do so. This would have given the client a chance to say "no." Rather, the peer counselor, ever so gently, *directed* him to do so. If the client had refused, the peer counselor would have continued to talk with him anyway, though with extreme caution.

DON: Well, okay. I guess I have nothing to lose. (*There is a short silence.*) Okay. It's on top of the refrigerator.

PEER C: Now it's easier to talk. Talking things out really does help. I know it doesn't seem that way to you right now, but emotions change, given time. I want you to know there is always someone you can talk with here, twenty-four hours a day. But I think you need more than that right now. Many people go to a professional counselor during major transitions, and it helps them. Also, there are some very good antidepressant drugs if that's needed. The therapist would know. You're going through a major transition right now. It is natural that you feel trapped, like there is no way out. But there really is. Have you ever been to a professional counselor?

DON: No. I can't afford anything like that. With just my income, I don't have enough to live on.

The peer counselor and the client discussed the client's insurance and found there was a possibility that it would pay some of the cost of therapy. Also, the peer counselor told the client about the mental health clinic, which charges on a sliding scale.

PEER C: I will help you get an appointment with a therapist, but you need someone with you right now. Do you have a friend or relative who would come be with you?

DON: I don't have relatives here, and I don't want to ask my friend. He's at work now.

PEER C: Would you go to him if he were in trouble?

DON: Well, sure. But I just can't call him and tell him about all of this.

PEER C: Would it help if I phoned him?

Don: Would you do that? Well, I guess that would be okay. I don't think any of this is going to work, but like you said, what do I have to lose?

The peer counselor got the name and phone number of the client and his friend and, on a second phone, called the friend, who agreed to take the client home with him for the night. The peer counselor told the friend about the loaded gun on top of the refrigerator and the two of them worked out a plan to get the client an appointment with a therapist. Then the peer counselor went back to the client and talked with him until the friend arrived.

Here is another example of a suicidal phone call, this time from a woman approximately 40 years old.

Peer C: Hello. This is the crisis line.

Edna: I need to talk to somebody.

Peer C: I'll be glad to talk with you.

Edna: Well, I'm not feeling very well. And I'm scared. I don't know what to do.

Peer C: You're scared and don't know what to do.

Edna: Yes. So much has happened. I just can't go on. Everything in my life is wrong. But now I'm scared.

Peer C: You say you can't go on. Tell me what scares you.

Edna: Well, I just wanted to end it all. But I feel so bad. And now I'm scared.

Peer C: Are you saying you tried to commit suicide?

Edna: Yes. And I think I am feeling sleepy. I'm so scared.

PEER C: I'm glad you called. I will work with you. But first I need to know where you are. What is your address? (*Client gives the counselor her full name and address.*) Edna, I'm going to get help for you. Can you go unlock your door and come back to the phone?

EDNA: Yes. I think I can. (*Brief silence*) I unlocked it.

PEER C: Edna, what did you take that is making you feel sleepy? Tell me exactly what you took and how long ago you took it.

EDNA: Diazepam. They are ten milligrams. Just before I phoned you.

PEER C: How many did you take.

EDNA: Don't know exactly. A handful.

PEER C: Edna, try to stay awake. You say you don't know how many you took? Was it more than ten?

EDNA: Don't know. So scared.

PEER C: I know you're scared right now. Hang in there. I'm going to get help for you, and I am going to stay with you. Where is the Diazepam bottle?

EDNA: Bathroom.

PEER C: Are you alone?

EDNA: Yes.

PEER C: I am going to use another phone and get help for you. Don't hang up your phone. I'll be right back. Do you understand that you are not to hang up the phone.

EDNA: Yes.

PEER C: (*Phones Emergency Services on another phone*) This is the crisis line. I have a woman on the other line who attempted suicide by taking ten milligram tablets of diazepam about ten minutes ago. (*Gives client's name and address*) She can't tell me how many pills she took. She says she is very sleepy. Her speech is slurred. The diazepam bottle is in her bathroom. She has unlocked the door to her apartment. (*Emergency Services indicates that assistance is on the way.*) Edna, help is on the way. Are you still there?

EDNA: Yes. I'm sleepy.

PEER C: Edna, do you have a phone by your bed?

EDNA: I'm sitting on the bed.

PEER C: Okay. That's fine. Stay on the phone with me. Try to stay awake. Help will be there soon.

The peer counselor stayed on the phone with Edna until the paramedics picked up the phone and said they would take charge.

Other Emergencies

Peer counselors deal with emergencies other than suicidal clients; for example, the physically abused, the homeless, the runaway teenager, and the client suffering from a drug reaction. Although the specific guidelines given above for dealing with a suicidal client are generally applicable for handling other emergencies, the latter vary so much that there is considerable room for ingenuity and improvisation on the part of the peer counselor. Outlined below are general guidelines for dealing with these other emergency situations; however, these will have to be shaped and honed on the spot by the peer counselor to fit specific emergency situations.

The first step is to *determine whether an emergency situation exists and, if so, the nature of the emergency.* The client does not always begin by telling us the true nature of her situation. A client whose family was thrown out of their apartment on a frigid winter day may tell us she, or her husband, needs to find a job. A woman who has just been raped may tell us she has been hurt and does not know whether to call her doctor. For this reason, in any contact with a client, we need to be attentive to the possibility of client needs that are not clearly expressed and that may indicate an emergency.

We should listen to our intuitive feeling that we may not be hearing the whole story. When we have suspicions, we need to check them out by shifting into our emergency mode of operation and immediately taking charge by being directive, asking questions, and giving instructions. Direct and specific questions are necessary, for example:

Physical Abuse
  "Are you in danger right now?"
  "Are you hurt or injured?"
  "Do you have cuts or bruises?"
  "Are you in pain?"
  "Have you seen a doctor?"
  "Do you have a safe place to stay tonight?"
Mental Health
  "Have you been to the mental health department?"
  "Can you afford to go to a psychologist?"
Shelter
  "Do you have a place to stay tonight?"
  "Where did you stay last night?"
  "Do you have friends you can stay with temporarily?"
  "Do you have money for shelter and food?"
  "Do you have a job?"
  "Have you stayed at a shelter before? When?"
Food and Financial Assistance
  "Are you a resident of this county?"
  "Have you been to social services?"
  "Do you have a job?"

"Do you have any food in the house?"
"Do you have any money to buy food?"

Although direct questions are necessary, we should avoid coming across like an attorney interrogating a witness. If the client wishes to tell her story or express her feelings, we should let her—but briefly, since time is of the essence. We also must attempt to gain the client's trust by letting our caring show through. The client who phones us in an emergency situation is usually highly emotional, disorganized, confused, and overwhelmed. It may take some effort to understand exactly what is going on with her. We need enough details to determine what kind of danger she is in and the immediacy of her needs. If our questions are off target, the client will let us know.

If the client is in imminent danger, our first responsibility is to *help her get out of danger*. This may include encouraging her to telephone for medical assistance or police protection or, if she is virtually incapacitated, making phone calls for help for her. Before we make calls for her, we need to gather whatever information the provider of the assistance will need, for example, name of client, age, approximate income, address (including apartment number), telephone number, number of children and their ages, and the client's exact needs. Before phoning a county or state agency, we need to know if she is a resident of the county or state.

If she is not in imminent danger but still needs something to be done at once, we need to *guide her toward doing what needs to be done immediately*. For example, once a client who has just been raped is sure she is no longer in danger from the rapist, she needs to get medical attention as soon as possible, to get treatment for her wounds, and to establish evidence should she decide to bring the case to court. We may need to encourage a client who has been battered by her spouse to leave her house immediately. She may also wish to contact the magistrate's office and take out a warrant against her abuser spouse. Usually the police will go back to her house with her to get her personal belongings.

If nothing must be done immediately, we need to *help her formulate a plan to abate the emergency*. This will include our determining what resources the client has for helping herself. She may, for example, have family or friends close by who could be of assistance. She may have a particular physician, therapist, or social worker who knows something of her situation and is available to help. We can help her clarify her thinking, decide her best course of action, and solicit needed assistance. If her level of functioning is such that she is unable to help herself, we may need to phone another person or agency for her. Depending on the resources available to our agency, we may be able to get another agency on a second line to advise us concerning the emergency. For example, if the client is reacting to a drug, the drug action agency can advise us as we go along, or we may want to get the client's number and have drug action phone her. The same may be true for rape crisis and runaway hot lines and the homeless shelter.

In general, we should stick with the client until we are reasonably confident that she can proceed further on her own or that she is in contact with needed assistance.

An Example of Dealing with an Emergency

In Chapter 8 we began a dialogue with a client, Nancy, who turned out to be in an emergency situation. Following is the entire session, which shows how to deal with an emergency.

PEER C: Hello. This is the women's center.

NANCY: Hello. I just need to talk to somebody.

PEER C: I will be glad to talk with you.

NANCY: Well, it's like this. My husband just left, so I can talk now. We've been having lots of trouble lately. Like, I mean he's got a bad temper and he gets real mad.

PEER C: Your husband gets real angry with you.

NANCY: Yeah. And I don't think I did anything wrong. (*Begins crying*)

PEER C: It's okay to take your time. I can tell you are very upset right now. (*Silence of about ten seconds*) You were saying your husband gets angry with you when you think you did nothing wrong.

NANCY: (*Screaming*) Yeah! And it hurts! It hurts! I'm bleeding. I think he broke my nose. What am I going to do? I'm bleeding all over.

PEER C: Okay, I'm going to help you. But first I need some information. Tell me where you are. What is your address? (*The peer counselor gets the client's name, address, and phone number so that if she becomes unable to talk, the counselor could phone for help or if she hung up could call her back.*) Okay, that's good. Nancy, we need to figure out how badly you are hurt. I need you to help me with this. Are you bleeding a lot? Do you feel like you might pass out?

NANCY: No. My nose is bleeding, but I don't feel like I'm going to pass out.

PEER C: Good. Now tell me how much you are bleeding?

NANCY: Well, I'm holding a small towel to my nose and there's a big spot on it. But my nose hurts terribly.

PEER C: Do you hurt anywhere except your nose?

NANCY: Well, my arm hurts too. I think it might be broken.

PEER C: We need to get you to the hospital or to your doctor as soon as possible. Is it all right with you for me to phone Emergency Services?

NANCY: No, I'd rather not do that. He's beat me up before and I didn't go to the doctor, only I think it's worse this time. I think I ought to go to my doctor. I think I can get there all right by myself.

PEER C: Tell me who you know who can help you. Do you have a relative, or a friend?

Nancy told the peer counselor of a friend who would drive her if she could get off work. The peer counselor asked Nancy for permission to phone the friend and tell her what had happened. Nancy replied that the friend already knew her husband was abusive. The counselor kept Nancy on the phone while she called the friend on the other phone. The friend said she would get her at once. The counselor went back to the phone, had Nancy unlock her door, and continued talking.

PEER C: It would be good if you tell your doctor exactly what happened. Then he can document the abuse just in case you need this record later. Nancy, I'm concerned for your welfare. You don't have to take abuse from your husband. Would you agree to go home with your friend after you've seen the doctor and phone us back so we can talk about what steps you can take next?

NANCY: Yes, I appreciate your support. I'll do that.

The peer counselor stayed on the phone with Nancy until the friend arrived. Later the counselor talked with the volunteer who took the next shift, telling her that Nancy might phone again. When Nancy phoned later in the day, the new counselor encouraged her to stay away from her house and explained that, if requested to do so, the police would go in with her to get her personal things. Nancy and the counselor discussed how she might approach her husband about obtaining professional therapy and, if he would not, how Nancy could become independent of him.

Notice that in the above case the peer counselor depended on Nancy to help decide whether or not this emergency demanded immediate intervention on the part of the peer counselor. The client has more information than we do and can often be helpful in evaluating the nature and extent of needed assistance. With Nancy, her relatively calm speech at the beginning of the session and her obvious ability to help make decisions were clues that only relatively minor intervention on the part of the peer counselor was required. If she had continued yelling and screaming that her nose and arm were broken, and the peer counselor had not been able to get any other information from her, the counselor would have phoned Emergency Services, assuming he or she was able to obtain Nancy's name and address. Notice also that the peer counselor did not phone Nancy's doctor, but wisely decided that Nancy, together with her friend, would be in a better position to judge the urgency and necessity for Nancy to get to a doctor and could relay this to the doctor's office.

Identifying the Client Whose Thinking Is Impaired

Another category of "special cases" is the client whose thinking is impaired by mental illness, drugs, debilitating depression, or other causes. Some of these clients live, either permanently or temporarily, in a world that is far removed from reality as we know it. We hear their words, but have little, if any, understanding of what they are thinking. They may see "visions" or hear "voices," their speech may be disjointed or slurred, their thoughts may seem unconnected or unrelated, they may make a sudden transition from one topic to another, and they may indicate a rapid heartbeat, drowsiness, or panic. Many of these clients are repeat callers and already are connected to a social worker, therapist, or substance abuse counselor who referred them to our agency to help them get through the difficult times between visits to the referring professional.

Other clients may speak in a slow, flat, emotionless voice, their tone indicating feelings of utter pessimism, rejection, dejection, and hopelessness. Such clients may exhibit additional classic symptoms of depression such as ongoing sadness and anxiety; an "empty" feeling; sleep problems or problems with eating and weight loss or gain; loss of interest or pleasure in ordinary activities, including sex; exhaustion; difficulty in concentrating, remembering, or making decisions; excessive use of alcohol; and thoughts of suicide or suicide attempts.

As peer counselors we are not expected to know the cause of impaired thinking. We are not expected to know the psychological labels for various mental conditions or to be able to identify a client as being mentally disturbed. Nor do we need to have an extensive knowledge of drugs and their effects or be able to determine whether a client's "crazy talk" is a reaction to a drug (including alcohol). The client's thinking may be mildly impaired, profoundly impaired, or anywhere between these two extremes. It is not essential that we determine with any great precision exactly where the client is on this continuum. But, because there are definite limits to our ability to be of assistance to a somewhat incoherent client, we do need to be able to recognize that our client's thinking is in some way impaired. If the indicators provided above prove insufficient for making a firm judgment, a single, simple clincher is that we cannot communicate with the client using our ordinary forms of communication. If we cannot, the client likely is not in a growth mode, and to respond to her as we would a typical client would probably be useless and could be counterproductive. (Contacts with impaired clients sometimes turn out to be emergencies. Emergencies were addressed earlier and are not repeated here.)

Dealing with the Impaired Client

Our goals when dealing with a client whose thinking is impaired are to connect her with a professional helper, if she is not already connected, and to help her cope with her immediate emotional pain. When referring a client to a professional, we may need to help make the appointment. This is particularly so with a severely depressed client because she may be incapable of taking the initiative to get help. She often believes there is no help.

Although some of our basic peer counseling skills are appropriate to use with a client whose thinking is impaired, asking questions, using direct statements, and sometimes giving instructions also are suitable. The more the client's thinking is impaired, the less likely we are to reach her on an intellectual level. We need to use caution in our choice of words. With a client whose thinking is only mildly impaired, a simple misunderstood comment can be clarified and the conversation continued. A misunderstood comment can come through as a threat to a client whose thinking is severely impaired, abruptly ending the conversation.

Attempting to communicate with a client whose thinking is impaired requires that we be patient, speak kindly and calmly, and try to build trust. Even if we cannot understand what she is trying to tell us, we can assure her that we are there to help if we can.

If we find, after staying with the client for a few minutes, that she has virtually no ability to communicate—if we cannot make any sense of what she is saying—we might ask if there is anyone with her with whom we can speak. If there is, he or she may be able to serve as interpreter. If not, our only recourse is to explain that we cannot understand her and are going to hang up. We can invite her to phone again or to have someone phone for her.

Most impaired clients, however, retain some ability to communicate. If we find some clarity in the client's discourse, we can provide whatever support seems appropriate. Situations concerning impaired clients are so varied that few specifics can be given on how to deal with them. However, the following general guidelines are applicable. (Keep in mind that we are referring here to situations that are not emergencies.)

- Do not reflect feelings unless the client states a feeling. We are not trying to help the client grow—just to help her get through the next few minutes.
- Do not go into details when responding to content. This might reinforce her negative thinking. At most, use brief summaries.
- Speak in a calm, kind, but authoritative voice:
  "I can tell you are having a really bad time right now. Can you tell me what is happening?"

  "Try to calm down and talk slowly."

  "Tell me how I can help you."
- If the client appears to be or tells us she is a substance user, avoid guiding her toward talking about how to quit. If she wishes to talk about quitting, let her initiate it.
- If the client tells us she is coming down off a drug, respond to her fear with reassurances of reality:
  "This line isn't tapped."

  "There is no alien from outer space trying to harm you. This perception is just from the drug you took. It will go away."

  "You are not losing your mind."

  "You are not going crazy."

  "You are not shrinking. It is only the effects of the drug."

These assurances may need to be repeated over and over. If the client wants to talk, make an effort to keep her talking about real things.

- In attempting to stabilize the client's distress, questions are in order:

  "Have you had any food today?"

  "Do you have a doctor or therapist?"

  "Are you taking medication?"

  "Have you taken your medication today?"

  "What does your doctor or therapist say to do at times like these?" (Note: The peer counselor should *not* phone the therapist or physician except in an emergency. Chances are that everything that can be done is being done for this client. The client may phone our co-workers every day with the same story.)

- Avoid guiding the client toward talking about her problem. This could prove frustrating to her, even detrimental in some cases. Instead, ask the caller to focus on her surroundings. Find out what kinds of tasks or diversion she could engage in to keep her mind occupied. Steering her to talk about her pet cat or dog, for example, often is successful in getting her away from her fearful thinking.

- Tread softly. Do not push. Do not say to the client, "Pull yourself together." Focus on doing no harm.

- Have compassion but not pity. If you feel pity, try not to let it show. (Pity is belittling.)

- Become familiar with the drug action agency, Alcoholics Anonymous, and the mental health agency in your community. If the client is not already connected to an appropriate community agency or professional, attempt to give her a referral.

- Do not expect too much of yourself. While peer counselors can help in many areas, we cannot do everything.

Some Examples of Dealing with the Impaired Client

Following is an example of a phone call to a crisis line from a 71-year-old female client, Loren, whose thinking was impaired.

PEER C: Hello, this is the crisis line.

LOREN: Everything has gone wrong today. I can't remember where I put it. I thought I put it right here. I had nightmares last night. That doctor said he would phone and he didn't. I think he ought to do what he said, don't you?

PEER C: You are having an unusually trying day.

LOREN: Yes. I don't think I will go back to that church anymore. None of them have been to see me in a long time. And they used to give me a little money now and then. And I once thought they cared. They don't care. Nobody cares. I may change churches.

PEER C: I don't believe I have talked with you before. You mentioned your doctor earlier. Are you taking medication?

LOREN: Yes. He gives me three kinds of pills. I don't believe they are helping. I think I may stop taking them.

PEER C: Have you had any food today?

LOREN: (*Answering obediently, like a child*) Yes, for breakfast I had a muffin and milk. Oh, these terrible cockroaches in my kitchen! My landlord said they would spray, but they have not. I don't know how much longer I can live in this hell hole. (*Screaming*) It's a *hellhole*! Hellhole! Hellhole! Oh, I can't stand it. Stand it! Stand it! Oh, what am I going to do? I would kill myself except my religion won't allow it.

PEER C: Have you taken your medication today?

LOREN: (*Calmly*) Let's see. (*Short silence*) I was supposed to take one at nine o'clock. Let's see, I was watching my TV program at nine o'clock. No, I forgot it.

PEER C: Why don't you go take it right now. I will wait.

LOREN: You won't go away?

PEER C: No, I will wait.

LOREN: (*After about three minutes client returns to phone.*) Okay. I took it. But that doctor said he would phone and he didn't.

PEER C: You mentioned that you watch TV. What programs do you like?

LOREN: I don't like any of them. Its just bad news all the time. The news programs get me so upset. The world is in such a mess. Nothing but crime. (*Screaming*) Oh, what's going to happen? To happen! To happen!

PEER C: Do you have a pet cat or dog?

LOREN: My little doggie, Sam. He keeps me going. He is so cute and smart. You should see him. And he tries to protect me. We go for walks. He loves the walks. I would be afraid to go out in this neighborhood without my little doggie, Sam. (*The client begins to lament about how unfriendly people are in her apartment building and how much crime there is in her neighborhood. The peer counselor brings her thoughts back to her pet dog by asking her how long she had it. Then, after about ten minutes*)

PEER C: Our time is up for now. You may phone us again sometime.

LOREN: Oh, thank you, thank you! You are so good. Goodbye.

Notice in the above dialogue that the peer counselor responded to content only briefly and selectively; she or he did not reflect feelings. The object of this conversation was to avoid rein-forcing the client's negative thoughts and to help her feel com-panionship for a few moments.

Following is an example of a phone call to a crisis line from a male, Peter, in his mid-forties.

PEER C: Hello, this is the crisis line.

PETER: (*Screaming*) No! No! I can't stand it! I am so scared! Please help me! Somebody please help me!

PEER C: I am here to help you. Try to calm down and tell me what's wrong.

PETER: (*Screaming, wailing, moaning, sobbing, shrieking*)

PEER C: (*Speaking loudly over all the commotion*) I can tell you are re-ally scared. I can't tell what is wrong, but I am going to stay right here. I'm going to stay on the phone with you. Do *not* hang up your phone. Remember, I'm right here. As soon as you are able, tell me what is wrong.

PETER: (*Continues to yell but manages to say*) It is going to get me. I'm going to die. I've got to get away.

PEER C: (*Very loud so as to be heard above the moaning*) You are scared you are going to die and feel you must get away. I am right here with you. (Note: At this point the peer counselor could not assure the client that he was not going to die because he or she did not know what was happening.)

The wailing went on for some time. The peer counselor contin-ued to assure the client that he or she was still there. The client took several deep breaths, then calmly explained that he has panic attacks. He cannot go out of the house without panicking. Today he grew tired of staying inside and decided to try to go out of the house. That was when the panic attack began. He rushed back into the house and phoned us. He explained that he was working with a therapist and making some progress. He thanked the peer counselor for staying with him and hung up.

Following is a dialogue between a peer counselor and Ruth, a new client at a Women's Center. They go into the counseling room. Ruth looks dejected. They are seated.

RUTH: I'm really having a rough time. I can't eat or sleep. Some days I can't go to work, I'm too tired, and when I do go, I don't do a good job, and everybody knows something is wrong.

PEER C: You can't eat or sleep, and your work is suffering.

RUTH: That's right. And there's nothing wrong. I have a loving family, a good job, and an understanding employer.

PEER C: You are saying there is nothing outwardly wrong and you don't know why you are feeling so disheartened.

RUTH: That's right. But I cry most of the time. I can't seem to stop. I can't do a good job with my children. My husband tries to understand, but our marriage is suffering. And I try, I really do. (*crying*)

PEER C: It's all right to cry. (*Waits a minute or two*) Ruth, how long have you been feeling this way?

RUTH: It started six months ago and just gets worse and worse. I don't know how long I can go on this way. I'm so miserable. I just dread getting up in the morning. Sometimes I don't get up.

PEER C: You have been feeling despondent like this for a long time. You mentioned that you don't know how long you can go on this way. I was wondering what you meant by that.

RUTH: There's no way out and I'm just making my family suffer. They would be better off without me.

PEER C: Are you thinking of suicide?

RUTH: Oh no, no. I wouldn't do anything like that. It's just that I can't seem to do anything for myself. Like it's out of my control.

The peer counselor listened and responded to content for a few minutes.

PEER C: Ruth, I hear you saying you are feeling helpless and hopeless right now. Many people have periods in their life when they feel despondent and discouraged and can't cope and, with help, are able to get back to being their old self. I'm not qualified to help you, but I can give you some good referrals. I admire you for coming in today. I know it took courage. Would you like us to go to the referral file and together make an appointment with someone who can help you?

Ruth: Well, if you really think there's a way out of this, I'll try whatever you say.

How Long Should We Talk with the Impaired Client?

If the client is frightened about a drug reaction or drug withdrawal, a relatively lengthy session may be constructive. If the impaired client called simply because she is scared, bored, or intoxicated, a much shorter session is appropriate. A good way to end a phone call is to say, "Our time is up, perhaps you can . . . [refer to some task or diversion talked about earlier]."

New peer counselors tend to be particularly moved by the suffering of the impaired client and tend to become overly invested in helping her. Such a client is often a repeat caller, and experienced peer counselors tend to become complacent with or even desensitized to her.

The impaired may be our most frustrating, and challenging, clients. It is difficult for us, who have had no training regarding mental illnesses or drug abuse, to see our way clearly when dealing with such a client. We listen to her words, but we cannot imagine how her brain works. It is difficult for us to refrain from applying our usual interpretations to her thinking and behaviors, even though we know these translations are inaccurate. Although this client may not feel the way we envision her to feel, she probably is a tortured soul. And human companionship and caring do help. We do need to spend time with her. My belief, though, is that peer counselors who discipline themselves to limit the time spent with this type of client give more quality help than those who cannot find a way to end the session after a relatively brief encounter.

Attempting to communicate via the intellect does not work very well with the impaired. But sometimes their hearts are open, and if ours are also, we can reach them that way. It is not so much what we say to these clients. When we are truly able to connect, both counselor and client know it.

An Introduction to Peer-Counseling the Dying

Peer counselors sometimes talk with clients who are grieving their own imminent death. Although we use basically the same skills that we use with other clients, there are a few extra guidelines and a few things it may be helpful for the peer counselor to know.

Emotions of the Dying

Elisabeth Kubler-Ross (1970) categorized the stages that people go through when they are faced with tragic news (i.e., coping mechanisms) as (1) denial and isolation, (2) anger, (3) bargaining, (4) depression, and (5) acceptance.

The client who is dying does not always go through all of these stages; if she does, she may not experience them in this particular order. She may even be in two stages at once, or alternate back and forth between stages, particularly between denial and acceptance. We do not tell the client about the five stages nor try to work with her regarding which stage she is in. She is not interested in stages that groups of dying people go through; she is concerned with her own, individual, unique process of dying. However, our knowing about the steps may help us better understand our client who is dying and thus increase our comfort and confidence levels as we attempt to minister to her.

Peer-Counseling the Dying

The person who is dying is not growing in the sense that she is trying to solve a problem, but she *is* growing. She has reached what surely must be the most monumental challenge in life: facing our own death, and accepting it as okay. We should respond to the content of what she says the same as we would with any other growing client. We should use the words "die" and "dying" when she uses them, and avoid using them when she does not. Our regular guidelines for reflecting feelings are appropriate: reflect feelings when she is struggling to make sense of her situation but is not highly emotional, and avoid reflecting when she *is* emotional.

We can expect that the client will tell her story repeatedly. This is a positive thing. It is her way of helping herself believe the truth. We should listen patiently to the repetitions and respond to content with each of them. We should not, cannot, rush her toward coming to terms with her death. Attempts to do so would only cause her to regress. She *must* be allowed to move at her own pace—

though having a warm, supportive listener no doubt frees her to progress more rapidly.

The client may believe her loss part of the time and deny it at other times. This is not senseless; it is the only way she can handle it. We should not challenge her by reminding her that, for example, "Yesterday you said you would not live much longer and today you are planning next year." Our job is to respond to content both times, even though one of her stories is diametrically opposite the other.

Sometimes the dying client will deny her death to the very end. This does not mean we, or she, have failed. She probably has done all she can bring herself to do. We must respect and accept her decision.

The dying client's religion is usually a prominent aspect in her attempts to cope with her own death. It may be a source of comfort or it may be a terror. We need to respect her beliefs, whatever they are. This may be hard for us. Our religion, if we are religious, may differ greatly from hers. To the extent that her religion is a source of comfort to her, we should be supportive of it. If it appears to be a negative factor in her coping, however, we should attempt to refer her to a professional therapist.

The dying client usually tires easily. When she appears tired, we might reflect this to her and see if she wishes to stop working. If we can afford the time, and if she wishes us to, we can share a silence with her while she rests. If she knows we are there, she may rest easier. Our slowing down our world to just "be there" can be particularly meaningful to her. Other than that, we can only patiently, warmly, and with caring listen, respond to content, and, when appropriate, reflect feelings. This is all we can do.

And this is a lot! Most of us experience anxiety when we are in contact with a dying person. A great deterrent to our doing a good job in peer-counseling a dying client is that most of us have not accepted our own mortality. It may be that we cannot, now.

Certainly the animal part of us strives to live. I believe that as we age our values change and accepting our mortality becomes easier. But few if any of us have really, honestly, completely accepted that we will die. In listening to a dying client, we are forcefully confronted with the reality of death. So we are trying to "be there" for our client at the same time we are dealing with our own emotions. This is not an easy combination. But if we are not there for her, then who? The dying client is often isolated from others—physically to some extent, and emotionally to a much greater extent. Often family and friends deny her impending death. They say, "Oh, don't think about that right now. You may get better. They are coming up with new cures all the time." This is understandable. Family and friends are going through similar stages of grief over the looming loss of their loved one. Often the client's health care providers either consciously or unconsciously avoid listening to her talk about her death. It makes them uncomfortable. They have not completely dealt with their own mortality. This is natural. Also, they cannot be all things to all people. But it further isolates the patient. So she is left, alone, to deal with the greatest challenge of her life. Not only is her body sick, she feels isolated and desolate. Her heart is lonely. Persons who are dying desperately need a supportive, unflinching listener. Peer counselors who do this are giving their client an extraordinary gift.

Epilogue

While peer-counseling guidelines are not to be taken lightly, each peer counselor must develop his or her own style. The guidelines for peer counseling delineated in this book are not intended to make all peer counselors alike or to prevent the peer counselor from being himself or herself. Some peer counselors are intense individuals; some are laid-back. Some are outgoing and friendly; others are more introspective.

Being our own person is what makes us valuable to the client. For the short time we are with the client, we are in a relationship with him. We will connect with the unique individual the client is, and he will connect with the unique individual we are.

Some peer counselors seem to have natural qualities—such as openness, intuitiveness, and a "third ear"—that make them, potentially, *good* peer counselors. Oddly enough, those who are not so endowed often make *better* peer counselors. When I was a child, I had a natural inclination toward music. Even before I could read music, I could hear a piece of music played on the piano and do a good job of simulating it. As a result, I was impatient and wanted to perform before I learned well. The outcome is that I never did learn to play the piano proficiently. Trainee peer counselors who have natural qualities that potentially would make a great peer counselor sometimes are too impatient to learn the basics.

No matter how talented a person is, playing it by ear is very limiting. Motivation for observing the guidelines comes from understanding the reasoning behind them. It is my hope that the material in this book has provided that reasoning. If we *learn the basics, our style will follow.*

References

Beattie, M. (1987). *Codependent No More*. New York: Harper & Row.

Benjamin, A. (1981). *The Helping Interview*. Boston: Houghton Mifflin.

Borysenko, J. (1987). *Minding the Body, Mending the Mind*. New York/Toronto: Bantam.

Kabat-Zinn, J. (1990). *Full Catastrophe Living*. New York: Dell.

Keith-Lucas, A. (1986). *Giving and Taking Help*. Chapel Hill, NC: University of North Carolina Press.

Kubler-Ross, E. (1970). *On Death and Dying*. New York: Macmillan.

Kushner, H. S. (1996). *How Good Do We Have to Be?* Boston/New York/Toronto/London: Little, Brown.

Lerner, H. G. (1985). *The Dance of Anger*. New York: Harper & Row.

Maslow, A. (1987). *Motivation and Personality*. New York: HarperCollins.

Raz, S. (1997). *Hasidic Wisdom: Sayings from the Jewish Sages*, trans. D. P. Elkins and J. Elkins. Northvale, NJ: Jason Aronson.

Richo, D. (1991). *How to Be an Adult*. New York/Mahwah: Paulist Press.

Rogers, Carl R. (1961). *On Becoming a Person*. Boston: Houghton Mifflin.

Tournier, P. (1964). *Why I Am Afraid to Tell You Who I Am*. New York/Evanston/London: Harper & Row.

Index

About the Author

Jewel Rumley Cox has worked for over twenty years as a volunteer peer counselor in various community agencies in Tallahassee, Florida and Raleigh, North Carolina. These agencies include a drug abuse prevention center, women's center, church, and crisis line. In a few hours each week, she has cumulatively peer counseled thousands of troubled women and men. In addition to peer counseling, her work included handling emergencies, referring clients to other community agencies and professionals, facilitating support groups, giving workshops, serving on planning committees, and training new volunteers to do peer counseling. She has attended peer counseling training in various volunteer agencies, first as trainee and then as trainer.

Mrs. Cox completed an intensive two-week, sixty-hour training course conducted by Stephen Ministries (an international nondenominational religious organization dedicated to training lay church members to counsel their peers), after which she founded a Stephen Ministry in a local church. This latter activity included interviewing and screening applicants and training lay care ministers to counsel their peers. Five years later, this ministry remains active, successful, and growing.

At The Women's Center of Raleigh, the author developed training materials and, for two years, led the team responsible for training new peer counselors. The training plan she devised for the center, which also is the basis for *A Guide to Peer Counseling,* was based on her observations regarding what a peer counselor DOES when he or she successfully counsels a peer. From this job analysis, she developed goals and objectives, and drafted a logical and thorough delineation of the skills necessary to meet those goals and objectives. These varied work experiences provided her with an understanding of what peer counselor training format works—and what does not work.

Mrs. Cox has received various volunteer awards including the 1984 Individual Human Service Volunteer Award, in appreciation and recognition of distinguished service to Wake County, NC. She resides in Raleigh with her husband, who is a retired research psychologist.